Befriending Life

ENCOUNTERS WITH HENRI NOUWEN

EDITED BY BETH PORTER

*with Susan M. S. Brown
and Philip Coulter*

Image Books / Doubleday
New York   London
Toronto   Sydney   Auckland

AN IMAGE BOOK
PUBLISHED BY DOUBLEDAY
a division of Random House, Inc.
1540 Broadway, New York, New York 10036

IMAGE, DOUBLEDAY, and the portrayal of a deer drinking from
a stream are trademarks of Doubleday, a division of
Random House, Inc.

Book design by Jennifer Ann Daddio

Permissions:
Excerpts from *Our Greatest Gift* by Henri J. M. Nouwen, copyright ©
1994 by Henri J. M. Nouwen. Reprinted by permission of
HarperCollins Publishers, Inc., New York.
Letters to Marc about Jesus by Henri J. M. Nouwen, copyright © 1987,
1988 by Henri J. M. Nouwen. English translation copyright © 1998
by Harper and Row, Publishers, Inc., and Darton, Longman & Todd,
Ltd. Reprinted by permission of HarperCollins Publishers, Inc.,
New York.
Sabbatical Journey by Henri J. M. Nouwen, copyright © 1998 by the
Estate of Henri J. M. Nouwen. Reprinted by permission of the
Crossroad Publishing Company, New York.
"Circus Diary—Part I: Finding the Trapeze Artist in the Priest" by
Henri J. M. Nouwen, copyright © by the Estate of Henri J. M.
Nouwen. Reprinted by permission of the *New Oxford Review*,
Berkeley, CA.

The Library of Congress has cataloged the hardcover edition
as follows:

Befriending life: encounters with Henri Nouwen;
edited by Beth Porter with Susan M. S. Brown
and Philip Coulter.—1st ed.
p. cm.
I. Nouwen, Henri J. M. I. Porter, Beth. II. Brown,
Susan M. S. III. Coulter, Philip.
BX4705.N87 B44 2001
282'.092—dc21
[B]
00-066008

ISBN 0-385-50203-6

September 2002
First Image Books Edition

1 2 3 4 5 6 7 8 9 10

To all those for whom Henri Nouwen's
ministry and writings have been a
source of life

Contents

A Biographical Sketch
of Henri Nouwen

Henri J. M. Nouwen was born in Holland in 1932 and ordained a Roman Catholic priest in the Diocese of Utrecht in 1957. He worked briefly as an army chaplain and as chaplain on a steamship carrying immigrants to America, but mainly he focused on further studies in psychology. These took him to the Menninger Foundation in the United States in 1964. In 1966 he accepted a position teaching psychology at the University of Notre Dame. He returned to the Netherlands to teach from 1968 to 1971, when he took a position teaching pastoral theology at Yale Divinity School. In the seventies he became increasingly concerned about conditions in Latin America. When he left Yale in 1981 he spent several months in Central and South America and then traveled widely in North America, speaking about the suffering and the inspiring faith of the people there. He took a position teaching at Harvard during these years. In 1985 he left Harvard and went to live for a year in the original L'Arche community in France, and the following year he became pastor of L'Arche Daybreak in Toronto, Canada. He died suddenly of a heart attack in the Netherlands on September 21, 1996, while en route to St. Petersburg for the making of a film about Rembrandt's famous painting *The Return of the Prodigal Son*. Two funerals were held, the first in the cathedral in Utrecht and the second in a cathedral in Markham, Ontario, near the Daybreak community. Henri wrote more than forty books, which have been translated into at least twenty-two languages.

Foreword

On Henri's sixtieth birthday in January 1992, the L'Arche Day-break community hosted a celebration of his life. Henri was like a child, excited and curious to know "the plan." But "the plan" was a surprise. He was simply to show up at the appointed time. When Henri arrived, his friend Robert Morgan, a professional clown, ushered him into a small room apart from the two hundred friends gathered in a huge circle to greet him. Robert, himself dressed as a clown, helped Henri into a clown suit and asked him to crawl into the clown bag open before him. Robert zipped the bag closed and dragged it, with Henri inside, out into the center of the circle.

Robert then began his routine of birthing. He referred to the being in the bag, and with each suggestion that a baby clown was soon to be born, there was a shuddering within the bag. Chuckles were heard as all began to catch on. The baby clown was reluctant to emerge. Robert spoke patiently, telling the clown that he appreciated his fear but that new and marvelous wonders awaited him if he could just find the courage to come out. Very tentatively, a huge bare foot appeared and pushed itself into the air, exposing a long, skinny, hairy leg. By now everyone was roaring with laughter. Slowly, Henri the clown emerged. The clown duo then performed together, inviting the captivated audience to engage and enter fully into their own lives. What was most touching was the way Henri so spontaneously jumped into the act and instinctively knew how to make the most of it!

His performance that night was a wonderful image of Henri's life. As a bestselling spiritual writer and Harvard and Yale professor, Henri had obviously made his mark in the world. But as many knew, his journey toward maturity and coherency had presented him with continual opportunities to choose life over fear, disillusionment, and feelings of rejection. Henri gradually completed some important passages from pain and darkness to light and hope, but he struggled with others, on and off, to the end of his life. Through it all, though, his embrace of life was total. He loved his life even though he suffered, and he lived his rebirths through sorrow with passion and compassion. His ministry became more and more fruitful as his life as priest, pastor, psychologist, lecturer, writer, and friend to many unfolded. He invited and encouraged others to welcome their challenges and to befriend their lives.

In one of his later books, *Our Greatest Gift*, Henri wrote about befriending death. He said that we could transform our death from our worst nightmare into our greatest gift for those we love. Now, five years after Henri's death, I see more fully the truth of his insight. I am surprised to recognize his passionate spirit energizing and motivating so many new and old friends, especially myself. He pushes us to recognize how special and precious our little lives are.

When I was given the manuscript of this collection and asked to write its foreword, I was amazed at the vibrancy and diversity of relationships and life experiences recounted. The forty-two contributions in *Befriending Life* all witness to friendship. They tell of both Henri's deep frailties and his great gifts, not so that we will emu-

late him but so that we will be inspired. By showing Henri's reluctance to accept some of the challenges of his own life journey,
these friends make him real, like us. By describing some of their
own agonizing or amusing resistances and surrenders, they help us
identify with them. By pointing to the ways friendship with Henri
taught them to give and receive support, they call us to do likewise.
Like Henri, like the clowns, and like these contributors, we laugh
and we weep. We live through dark times and difficult passages,
and we are inspired to recognize and appreciate more fully the
unique and precious story that belongs to each of us.

Henri used to insist that we read good spiritual books. He in-
structed us to read not out of curiosity but out of our profound
yearning, listening for something that corresponds to the inner ur-
gencies of our lives. He summoned us to read in order to learn
more about the meaning of life, to deepen in love and wisdom. He
would tell us, "Chew on the word. Let the word enter into your
flesh and your heart. Don't let your head move you too quickly
through the contents, but let your desire help you identify and
grasp the deep meaning of the word. Open yourself, and let the
word compel you and become part of you. Let it touch and moti-
vate your life."

Befriending Life, read in this way, will surely touch that privileged
place in each of our hearts, calling us forth, like Henri the clown,
beyond our reluctance and fear into the wonder, the pain, and the
joy of rebirth in our deepest spirit.

Sue Mosteller, C.S.J.
Literary Executrix of the Henri Nouwen Estate
Henri Nouwen Literary Centre
L'Arche Daybreak, Toronto, Canada
April 2001

Preface

In the years immediately following Henri's death, many of his friends expressed the desire to write about his impact on their lives. In time, Sue Mosteller and I began to think about creating a collection of such stories. I felt delighted, honored, and a little daunted when Sue proposed that I take on this project.

At first, we thought the pieces in this collection would all be from people who knew Henri during the last ten years of his life, the years with us at L'Arche Daybreak. But after reflection we decided to expand the vision, and we sought out contributors with particular representative windows onto Henri's life and ministry. Thus, as well as contributions from Daybreak members and friends, the book includes memories from people who knew him in his native Holland, in his early years in the United States at the Menninger Foundation and Notre Dame, and in his years at Yale and Harvard Divinity Schools. Others recall his social justice concerns, his path as a writer, his travels, and his continual searching for a spirituality for our time. Some contributors can neither read nor write; others have advanced academic degrees. Some knew Henri for decades, others met him only briefly.

We asked the contributors not to eulogize Henri but to write about him as the complex person he was. Some of the pieces here are anecdotal, others are deeply personal accounts of Henri's spiritual guidance, and a few are reflective essays. We avoided presenting the pieces chronologically or according to subject, preferring to offer them as a multifaceted portrait. It might be helpful to think of the book as a musical composition—variations upon a theme, with certain melodies recurring, developed a little differently each time: Henri's gift of presence, his insight, his anguish and restlessness, his caring and faithfulness, his love of the Eucharist, his aesthetic sensibility. The full resonance of the collection unfolds gradually and with reflection.

To understand the context of many of these pieces, readers will need to know a little about L'Arche. In the communities of L'Arche (French for "the ark," as in Noah's ark), people with developmental disabilities (core members) and those who come to help them (assistants) live together as brothers and sisters, each contributing to the well-being of the others. The Beatitudes (the text from the Sermon on the Mount that speaks of the poor as blessed) are at the heart of L'Arche spirituality. Not all of us can do much of a practical nature, but each person has gifts to offer. Sometimes the gift is a peaceful spirit, as Henri discovered in Adam Arnett. Sometimes the person's need is the gift, calling forth another's compassion.

L'Arche Daybreak, founded in 1969 and the oldest L'Arche community in North America, is located in Richmond Hill, on the outskirts of Toronto, Canada. Daybreak has strong Anglican and Roman Catholic roots, but, like all L'Arche communities, it is open to people of all faiths or no particular faith. Besides homes, work settings, and day programs, Daybreak has the Dayspring, originally a small retreat house with a chapel. Now in a new chapel building, the Dayspring is both the spiritual center of the community and a work of outreach to the wider society, seeking to spread L'Arche's message that every person is of immense value.

To us at Daybreak, Henri Nouwen was friend and pastor, and his gifts were manifold—he loved us, he loved God, he loved life, and he listened well and offered us valuable spiritual insight. He suffered the trials of community life as intensely as any one of us. His fame was sometimes a liability to us, but his neediness was not; perhaps we loved him the more for it—for being at times both the most wise and the most broken among us. Henri taught us to remember those who had died by telling stories about them. Henri stories abound at Daybreak and, told with humor and gratitude, they are a source of joy and wisdom. We hope the stories here will be a source of joy and wisdom for all who read them.

Acknowledgments

I am enormously grateful to Sue Mosteller for her constant support and encouragement in the preparation of this book. I am also thankful to the L'Arche Daybreak community, especially the members of the Seniors' Program and Nathan Ball, community leader at the time, for freeing me for this work. And I want to express my appreciation to the many friends and community members who have encouraged me in it.

I cannot thank Susan Brown and Philip Coulter enough for the many hours they have given to this project and for the great spirit in which we have worked together as colleagues and friends. Susan was Henri's last editor, working closely with him from 1995 to 1996 and on his posthumously published books. Her judgment on many small and large editorial issues has been invaluable. Philip brought the objectivity of someone who did not know Henri but, as a Canadian Broadcasting Corporation producer, has broad communications experience. He also has an understanding of L'Arche, derived from working with L'Arche's founder, Jean Vanier, on his bestselling book *Becoming Human*.

Besides her editorial work on the contributions, Susan found most of the quotations from Henri's writings that we have placed through the book. The idea of including Henri's voice in this way was Philip's. He commented early on that in many tribute volumes the guest of honor is absent. Henri could not have borne to be absent!

Special thanks go to Maureen Wright, Kathy Christie, and Mary Lou Daquano of the Henri Nouwen Literary Centre for their patience, kindness, and practical support. Kathy, who knew most of the contributors from her work with Henri, helped in the early stages of the project. Maureen, the centre's administrator, handled many details, including the extensive communication with the publisher.

I express our gratitude to Linda Gustafson, who designed the inspiring initial package. Thank you to those who kindly made photos and drawings available from their personal collections. As well, I am grateful to Anne Kingsmill, Francis Maurice, Gabrielle Fraschetti, Ben Carniol, and Toni Urbanski, who gave practical assistance at important points in the preparation of the manuscript. And I am deeply appreciative of the continuous interest and support of many friends, especially Joe and Mary Egan. Joe and Mary also read the entire manuscript and offered helpful suggestions.

I want to thank Eric Major, Vice President and Publisher, Doubleday Religious Publishing Division, Trace Murphy, Senior Editor, and Siobhan Dunn, his able editorial assistant, for their enthusiastic reception of this book and their support of its publication.

Finally and especially, I express our gratitude to those who so generously wrote for this collection. I have felt deeply privileged to work with them throughout the editing process. I have appreciated their patience and openness, and I have been touched by what they shared. This book has been a labor of love, overused as that expression may be, and I believe this is as true for each one who contributed as it is for those of us who compiled it.

Beth Porter
L'Arche Daybreak,
Toronto, Canada

Befriending Life

A Conversation
with Henri

JACKIE RAND

*Jackie Rand, with her husband, Baruch, was a friend of the L'Arche Day-
break community and a member of the Kehillah Ahavat Hesed, the small
Toronto synagogue some Daybreak members attend. She was a social worker
and family therapist and also worked with people with AIDS. Jackie passed
away shortly before this book went to press. Baruch continues their friendship
with Daybreak.*

I met Henri Nouwen only once, at a soiree held by a Daybreak
friend in the spring of 1995. When my husband and I came into
the elegant home where my friend was living at the time, a number
of people were semiformally milling about with appetizers. She introduced me to a tall man in a dark suit jacket. We started what I
thought was a casual conversation, but quickly I realized I was engaged in a very unusual experience. I think it was because I felt en-
veloped by Henri's gaze, the object of his undivided attention to
the exclusion of everyone else. I have seldom had this sensation—
only in intimate conversations or with a therapist. Yet here was this
man I didn't know offering me the gift of his completely focused
attention. I had no idea who Henri was. When I was introduced, I

gathered that he was a priest, but I knew nothing else about him except that he was in some way involved in L'Arche Daybreak. At that time I knew very little about L'Arche itself.

Just to make conversation, I asked Henri what he was planning to do during the coming summer and was astonished by his reply. He said he was planning to rejoin a circus troupe in Germany and travel with them while he studied their way of life. When I asked him what prompted him, a priest, to such an unlikely undertaking, he said, "You have to understand that I regard circuses very highly. The best circuses, such as Cirque du Soleil from Montreal, teach me a great deal. They've taught me more than anything else about trust." Here Henri explained how in the trapeze act the flyer must allow himself to fly in the direction of the catcher without grasping, and it is the catcher's responsibility to connect without hurting or injuring the flyer. This requires infinite artistry and precision, and transparent trust. Unless the trapeze artists resolve all problems, doubts, or difficulties between them every day, this ability to connect within a split second becomes flawed and can lead to a fall.

In addition to the beautiful work of the trapeze artists, Henri would observe the circus community as a whole. He said, "I'm very much interested in understanding the workings of this circus community so I can apply my learning to the communities I am involved in, especially L'Arche. All the elements I need to learn are there in the circus: above everything, caring and trust and the ability to take risks without fear because of this caring and trust."

The skill of this completely charismatic stranger in combining philosophical and theological ideas with popular entertainment had for me the force of a parable. Had his ideas been expressed only conceptually, they could have been sterile and dry. Yet as he presented them, they were vivid and utterly engaging. He never seemed to be talking about religion, yet he was talking at a deep spiritual level.

I remember that Henri and I also spoke about the practice of meditation. I was meeting at the time with a meditation group that included some other guests at that party, but I was just a beginner. Henri was acquainted with both Eastern-style and Christian meditation. He demonstrated, taking a huge breath, what it would be like to take in a word that conveys a powerful concept—like *love* or *shalom* or a line from a prayer—to fill oneself with this healing quality breath after breath. This approach, according to him, was different from the detachment and peace sought in Eastern meditation. In his acceptance of both approaches and his clear explanation, he widened my understanding of what is possible in meditation.

My conversation with Henri took only fifteen minutes or so, but it was intense and I was even a little embarrassed by the exclusion of others—not deliberately but because we were communicating so authentically. When we parted and went on to chat with other guests, I felt that I had stepped out of a circle of light and deep significance back into the mundane world. Only later did I find out about Henri's achievements and renown. All I knew was that I had been in the presence of a very special human being.

God's Restless Servant

BOB MASSIE

Bob Massie, author, Episcopal priest, environmental and social justice activist, wrote Loosing the Bonds: The United States and South Africa in the Apartheid Years. *He directs CERES, the Coalition for Environmentally Responsible Economies, a national U.S. organization based in Boston, Massachusetts, through which environmental groups and institutional investors, including churches, promote greater accountability for large corporations. Bob met Henri at Yale.*

When I met Henri Nouwen I had never heard of Henri Nouwen, his books, his courses, or his fame. It was early September 1978, I was twenty-two years old, and I had just arrived at the orientation retreat for incoming students at Yale Divinity School. From my first moment at the windswept retreat house on Long Island Sound, I knew that I was in some different sort of place, where warmth and laughter and hospitality flowed with unsettling abundance.

At one point early in the weekend, someone suggested that a group of us swim out to a clump of rocks about a hundred yards from the beach. We arrived, clambered up, and someone began to sing. After several moments I noticed a tall, skinny man sitting next to me, his arms wrapped around gangly legs. He had pale skin, thinning hair, and active eyes. I said hello. He introduced himself as Henri. I almost didn't catch his name because he had an accent that swallowed some of his vowels.

I ran into this fellow periodically during the weekend, and eventually I noticed that other students were treating him with a touch of deference. Over supper I finally asked him who he was. He said simply that he was a Catholic priest. I didn't quite know how to react. There had been a Roman Catholic church across the street from the Episcopal church I had attended as a child. My Catholic friends had told me about some of their complicated rules and practices. But I had never before talked to an actual priest.

Thus began a friendship that stretched over eighteen years. By the time he died, Henri was such an important part of my life that I could not conceive that we would ever be out of touch. He had known me while I was a student; I had helped him with a number of his books; he had formed friendships with my family; he had been present at my ordinations to the Episcopal diaconate and priesthood; he had participated in all the major liturgical moments in my life; he had helped me through two of my most painful traumas; and he had offered spiritual and material support at critical moments without hesitation or reproach. Because I had lived with a range of health problems, for many years we both believed that he would outlive me. When I became a parent, I once asked him to take on a special task. If anything happened to me, I said, would he be willing to sit down and convey some of the nature and depth of my faith to my children? He solemnly vowed to do so. It never occurred to us that *I* might be in the position of explanation and interpretation after *he* had died.

To return to those first days at Yale Divinity School, I had taken a fairly long adolescent detour away from the Episcopal Church, in which I was raised, and had been deeply perplexed about faith. Only a year before, in the summer of 1977, I unexpectedly had an experience of Christ's presence and God's love and forgiveness so strong that I have never doubted God's existence since. I had returned to college, where I found that few people felt comfortable talking about religious conviction of any kind, and I ended up at Yale Divinity School for what was, in many ways, a foolish reason—the desire to be with people who could discuss Christianity without awkwardness.

In those first weeks I was hungry to learn about what it meant to be a follower of Christ. I had had an experience of Christ, yes, but I knew nothing about theology, liturgy, or church history. I knew nothing about prayer or the daily rhythms of a life of faith. Within a day or two someone—perhaps it was Henri himself—invited me to attend Henri's daily Eucharist, which took place in a small chapel directly below Marquand Chapel. I went with trepidation; I had been to only one Catholic service before. Soft light from two small windows near the ceiling streamed into the octagonal room. Every sound deepened and echoed off the massive stone walls. As people entered, they left the chatter of life outside. The gentle grace with which Henri led the liturgy testified to its familiarity and importance in his life. He invited people to join him in reading Scripture, in leading prayers. His dignity and his quiet made us feel welcome.

Henri read Scripture more slowly than any human being I have heard. He often read a short phrase and then left an immense pause.

"I am the vine. . . .

You are the branches."

Henri treated each phrase as important, and his very attention seemed to bring new life to phrases that had seemed too familiar to be powerful.

"From everyone to whom much has been given . . .

much will be required."

After he finished reading, he would speak. And listening to Henri preach in a small setting was unforgettable. In thinking about how to describe it, I keep returning to the statement used by people who heard Jesus: "He spoke as one with authority." It was not the authority of power or office; it was not the rhetoric of brilliant assertion, which forced conclusions on the listeners. He had the authority of clarity, vulnerability, and truth. He was able to do what Jesus did—to take the smallest encounters, the simplest experiences, and the most common human flaws, and cast them in a light which revealed them as vehicles for the grace of God.

For example, Henri once talked to us about the importance of cultivating a sense of gratitude in the spiritual life. Yes, I'm sure we all thought, yes, that's a good idea. We should definitely feel more gratitude.

But how does one do this, asked Henri. Gratitude seems to be an involuntary reaction. If this is so, how does one *discover* more gratitude in one's heart? That one had us stumped. If I had been forced to respond, I would have said that it was important to realize how much more we had than other people or some such variation on gratitude through guilt.

"The key to gratitude is to cultivate a sense of surprise. Surprise!" said Henri. We looked at each other.

"Let's say I call you up and say that I am coming over soon and I am bringing you flowers," he continued. "You might be very happy. You also might build up expectations about when I would get there and how nice the flowers would be. Indeed, you might build up such a strong sense of what was going to happen that when I actually got there and had only three daisies you might even be disappointed.

"But imagine instead that I call you and say that I will be coming by and then, when you open the door, there I am standing with a bunch of flowers. Surprise! I have brought you a gift that you didn't expect. You would be touched and happy . . . and grateful."

This idea, so deceptively simple and transparent, set off an internal reflection that has stayed with me for two decades. I look at myself, at the people around me, and at the way our ambitions and our culture goad us to ever higher expectations, and thus ever deeper resentments, and I realize that Henri's example is radical.

Some people, including some of the faculty in the schools where he taught, were uncomfortable with the simplicity of Henri's words. We live in an era of interpretation, of deconstruction. Nothing is what it seems; everything contains an element of irony and betrayal. The challenges of the world are challenges of the intellect—how to peel back layers of meaning, how to trump the unwitting enthusiast.

There is, of course, joy in the intellect, a joy that Henri understood well. I remember the pleasure of learning all the different ways theological words and deeds could illuminate each other; how the Eucharist could be understood through its Jewish roots, its early history, its extensive treatment in Protestant, Catholic, and Orthodox writings. Yet even as my intellect came to appreciate the strata and nuances, my heart longed for something direct. I enjoyed gaining knowledge *about* God through elaborate mental schemes. But I still wanted to know God in a way that went beyond verbal paradox, in a way that a hand brushes another hand in the dark.

And Henri made this possible. I am not quite sure how he did, except that it was a gift of the Holy Spirit. He succeeded partly because he did not fear simplicity and repetition. Instead of laminating new layers of clever interpretation on top of each other, he presented the Gospel as simply as possible. His life and his language were full of basic gestures and images, as one can see in the titles of his writings. The spiritual life was lived *With Open Hands.* Prayer was not a matter of mind but *The Way of the Heart.* Ministry was not about power, it was a commitment to *Reaching Out.* A life of faith was not a heroic act of the will but a continuous response to Jesus' question *Can You Drink the Cup?*

Henri, in person, conveyed a physical concreteness, an immediate energy that riveted his listeners. His voice had an immense range of intensities and moods—playful humor, wise admonishment, passionate urgency, quiet reflectiveness. He could be wonderfully self-deprecating. Once with several students he began talking about dreams. "Do you dream in English or in Dutch?" someone asked. Henri smiled. "In English," he said, "but with a little Dutch accent."

Little Dutch-isms popped into his speech and writing all the time. In his preaching about Jesus' time in the desert, Henri often described the three temptations as the temptation to be powerful, the temptation to be spectacular, and the temptation to be relevant. He always pronounced it with a great rolling Dutch *r* and soft *v*—*rrrrrrrrellephant.* He told me about a time he had been giving this talk to several hundred people in a large hall with a poor sound system. Afterwards, as often happened, people rushed to speak to him. One woman, visibly moved, came up to him and said, "Oh, Father Nouwen, thank you for those spiritual insights. You know, honestly, I had never thought about it before, but as you spoke your words pierced my heart. You are absolutely right. I do indeed feel the temptation to be an elephant!"

When Henri's voice became animated, so did his hands. Each

finger looked like it was about nine inches long. They were wide, with great, flat fingernails. His thumbs were equally immense, so that when he spread out all ten fingers, which he often did, he looked briefly like a tree frog. And the fingers were always active. When he was trying to express something, he would rub them together, pointed upward, as though attempting to balance a marble on the tips. His squeezing, tugging gestures made it look like he was striving to milk meaning directly out of the air. He would point his fingers down and rotate his wrists as though trying to stir a separate little pot with each digit. His fingers were as much an instrument of communication as his voice; they were a ten-member liturgical dance corps that performed in front of him whenever he opened his mouth. He spoke, and they swirled through the air, coming together in reverence, flinging apart in exuberance. During the Eucharist, when he raised the consecrated host above his head, his fingers looked like they were carrying someone on their shoulders.

When I saw Henri in his coffin, I felt the physical reality of his death not just because his face was quiet and his eyes closed but because his hands were still.

Everyone who read Henri's work knew something about his inner struggles; indeed, the grace of God that flowed through Henri was directly related to his ability to share his weakness with his readers and his friends. Though the Bible is full of flawed servants who berate themselves for their weaknesses—Abraham, Moses, and Isaiah come to mind—most religious writers still slip easily into pietistic exhortation, and most readers expect this. Henri was different. He started by conceding his flaws—his loneliness, his restlessness, his desire for friendship, his jealousy, his uncertainty—which he managed to do without slipping into psychological exhibitionism. His ability to understand and share the love of

"A ten-member liturgical dance corps."

God was rooted in awareness of his dependence on the grace of God. He described this in detail in his book *The Wounded Healer.* But it is one thing to understand something in the mind and quite another to live it out in one's life.

For example, as many people have written, there was a restlessness deep in Henri's heart that kept him moving from place to place, person to person, community to community. It jumps out of the pages of some of his books, but it was even more palpable in person. That restlessness came across sometimes as awkwardness, sometimes as impatience, sometimes as petulance. Once he was delighted when my son Samuel, who was about eight, came and sat next to him on the couch. Henri began peppering Samuel with a breathless stream of questions: "So, Sam, how are you doing? How's school? What do you like to learn? Do you have any favorite games?"

Samuel looked at me with some anxiety and said, "Daddy, is this a kind of interview?" No, I reassured him, Henri was just trying to learn about his life. But Samuel retreated a bit and later politely withdrew from the room. Henri looked at me with sadness. "I just don't know how to talk to children," he said.

This pattern of Henri trying to engage someone, being disappointed that the person could not fulfill his expectations, and experiencing rejection because the person withdrew was something that many of Henri's friends experienced. At one point, when I was still at Yale, Henri protested that the students with whom he was friends never included him in their social events. "Why don't you ever just call me up and ask me to go to the movies?" he said.

"You want to go to the movies?" I asked.

"Yes, of course," he replied. "That's what friends do."

So from then on I called him up whenever a bunch of us were headed out to the movies. But he was always busy or too tired.

Finally, in exasperation, I said, "Henri, do you remember when you said that friends invite each other to the movies?"

"Yes," he responded.

"Well sometimes, Henri, when a friend invites someone to the movies, the other person actually says yes."

He looked troubled, then laughed. From then on it was much less complicated to maintain a balance.

Looking at Henri's life as a whole, it is easier to see how God may have used his restlessness to benefit all of us. Henri became an explorer who entered people's lives and then went out, almost on their behalf, to meet others. Everywhere he went he created new connections between people, he opened up new opportunities. Henri was our emissary into communities and places that were beyond the reach of our constrained lives and imaginations. Sometimes when I think about Henri I am reminded of Paul the Apostle, who could have remained a prominent, privileged leader in one corner of the world but whose encounter with Jesus flung him to the distant reaches of the earth.

But for those who knew and loved him well, Henri's restlessness was a source of concern, exasperation, even anger. When I worked on *¡Gracias!* with him in the summer of 1982, he had been asking for about a year whether God was calling him to live in South America. My own view was that the answer was probably yes. So when Henri called to tell me that he was planning to move from Yale to Harvard Divinity School, I couldn't believe it. I repeated to him all the things he had just said to me. Henri told me he was certain that this was what he wanted to do, partly because the liberation theologian Gustavo Gutiérrez, whom Henri much admired, had said that he would be more useful to the poor people of Latin America if he maintained a connection with an elite institution like Harvard. I could understand the reasoning, but I worried that Harvard would only offer more of the difficulties that Henri had encountered at Yale. I told him so. He reassured me, not very convincingly, that he had taken this into account.

Henri made a valiant effort at Harvard. But neither he nor Harvard really understood each other; each was looking for the wrong thing in the other. Harvard was looking for a kind of star power that would enliven—but not offend—the community. Henri was looking for an institutional equation that would allow him to resolve all the contradictions in his life—his desire for both

prominence and hiddenness, his desire to be both bold and accepted, his desire alternately to embrace and to challenge Roman
Catholic teaching. At Harvard, however, everyone challenges everyone else about everything, which means too often that people retreat into solipsistic safety. It's not an easy environment for
someone who wants to speak clearly about his or her personal experience of the love of God.

So after two and a half years, Henri left. Over the next few
years he mailed me a steady stream of new books; I sent him mes-
sages and birthday greetings (he was sensitive when people forgot).
We spoke regularly on the phone and, very occasionally, in person.
Mostly I worried about him from afar. Then came the winter of
1986, when I invited him to go to Russia.

A group from the Orthodox Church in America was planning
a visit as the Orthodox Church there prepared to celebrate one
thousand years of Russian Christianity in 1988. Henri had often
told me that he wanted to visit Russia, so when I found out there
might be an opening on the trip I called him immediately. He
sounded frighteningly tired. He didn't know. He would call me
back. A few days later he did. It turned out that he was about to
move to L'Arche Daybreak. So in order to go to Russia he would
have to fly to Canada, leave his possessions, then immediately depart with us for two weeks. Whatever you like, I said. There was a
silence. Then Henri said something that took me a while to understand. "I need to go," he said, "because I need to see the *Prodigal Son.*"

I soon realized that he was referring to the great painting by
Rembrandt that hangs in the Hermitage Museum in St. Petersburg. I called my mother, an expert on Russian culture who is
friends with many museum curators. "Tell Henri that he will be

able to spend as much time with the *Prodigal Son* as he wants," she said. So we flew to Russia.

It was a peculiar trip, full of unexpected poignancy and grace but also of encounters with the heavy hand of the Soviet state. I recall our visit to one particular church: a powerful experience, full of spirit, yet Henri did not seem able to receive it. He was physically exhausted. He seemed lost and uncomprehending, practically like a child. We had to make sure that he woke up on time, that he ate, that he got on the bus, that he stayed with the group. On occasion the confident, happy Henri came through, but in our private conversations it became clear that he was struggling with many uncertainties and unhappinesses.

Looking back, it seems as though Henri was enduring some sort of final spiritual test as he prepared to commit himself to life at Daybreak. He seemed trapped in the house of fear about which he had spoken so many times. After all his travels, he desperately needed and wanted a home. Despite his hundreds of friends, he fervently wanted to find a community. He wanted to be more of a living example of the words that had poured from his mouth and hand. He was terrified of disappointment. It was almost as though Daybreak were his last chance.

Yet toward the end of the trip his demeanor changed. We arrived in St. Petersburg and he was finally able to see the painting. I was with him, and, to tell the truth, I was perplexed. The painting struck me as odd and dark. For Henri, however, it was a window into the love of God. He approached it with modesty and awe. I almost expected him to step forward and merge with the kneeling figure, the lost and beloved son receiving the embrace of the joyful father. Over the next several days Henri spent so many hours with the painting that the museum gave him a chair so he could sit directly in front of it. He sat with it silently as groups of tourists wandered by, as the sun moved slowly across the walls. And after each visit he came back with more energy, more light in his eyes. When we returned to the United States he seemed ready for the new life ahead of him.

Once again, I and many other friends of Henri's held our breath. Would Daybreak be the home that he wanted? Or would we soon be hearing that the relationship had dissolved in disappointment, that he had packed his bags and set off again in search of a community that would love and understand him? I know the transition was not easy. Henri still had a long way to walk through the valley of the shadow of death. But it also soon became clear that in Daybreak he had found what he was looking for. On a superficial level Henri lost his formerly exasperating assumption that clothes would wash themselves, meals materialize out of nothingness, and houses do their own housework. Through his relationship with Adam Arnett and others he came to understand the physical demands of caring. More deeply, it seemed that he had finally found a community who could celebrate his great gifts without being frightened of his great needs—in other words, a family.

What impressed me in those last years was Henri's continued desire to grow. Instead of becoming comfortable with his prominence or resigning himself to unhappiness, he constantly pushed himself—and others—to reevaluate life and take on less predictable challenges. I experienced this directly. In the early 1990s, after spending six months in South Africa watching the rebirth of democracy, I wondered on my return to the United States whether I should run for public office. I struggled for months with the decision, trying to discern whether it was a temptation or a calling. I delayed telling Henri because I feared that he would not understand or approve. When I finally called him to share my thoughts, he excitedly congratulated me. Astonished, I laid out some of the reservations and hesitations that had troubled me. He brushed them aside. "If we waited until our vision or our motives were perfectly clear," he said, chuckling, "we would never get anything done. God asks us to step forward full of doubt, Bobby." He followed up our phone conversation with a letter making the same point and then, a few weeks later, with a generous campaign contribution.

During that period we would meet from time to time and talk over lunches that lasted several hours. He wondered about the directions his life and writing might take, and he even once speculated about whether he might someday leave the priesthood. It didn't come across as a loss of confidence in his vocation; the question presented itself more as "I wonder if, after forty or fifty years of service, God might draw me to some new forms of commitment." He talked about new insights and friendships he was forming. He talked, as he often did, about finding ways in which he could deepen friendships, but there was less guilt or neediness in his voice. He seemed to have gained a new footing against old demons.

The last time I saw Henri was on June 8, 1996. Fourteen years before, he had come to Louisiana to preach at my first wedding. When that marriage ended after more than a decade, Henri had helped me through my despair. When, through God's grace, I found a new partner, Henri came especially to meet her, and when Anne and I decided to marry, he made yet another trip, to New Jersey, to be part of our service. He read from a passage in Second Corinthians:

That is why we do not waver; indeed, though this outer human nature of ours may be falling in decay, at the same time our inner humanity is

renewed day by day. For we are well aware that when the tent that
houses us on earth is folded up, there is a house for us from God, not
made by human hands but everlasting, in the heavens. (2 Corinthians
4:16, 5:1)

The reception that followed was hot and giddy. In the middle
of the swirling clouds of people, Henri came up to me. Even in my
exhilaration I noted that his face was pale and fatigued. While
loud, happy voices careened around us, he leaned toward me and
said that he was leaving that evening on a flight to Europe, that he
was not feeling well, that he thought he should return home to rest.
Of course, I said, thank you for coming. It meant a great deal to
all of us that you were here. I would see him after summer vaca-
tion, surely; perhaps Anne and I would come to Daybreak. Yes, yes,
he said. That will happen. Peace be with you both. We embraced.
He turned and the crowd swallowed him.

Three months later, on September 21, 1996, Anne and I were
in church as members of the congregation stood up and offered
their usual intercessions and thanksgivings. I was leaning down and
looking at the floor when I heard someone say simply, "I would
like to give thanks for the life and work of Henri Nouwen."

Eighteen years before the name had meant nothing. But now
the name—and the unmistakable meaning of the words that surrounded it—unleashed a flash flood of images and emotions. It
took me a while to find out the details of what had happened. I
shuddered at the strange symbolism that his death had occurred as
he was on his way to St. Petersburg to revisit the *Prodigal Son*. But
even as I read the news stories and testimonials, I simply could not
believe he was dead. Even when I flew to his funeral, even when I
saw and touched his body in the casket, even when I witnessed the

waves of mourners and heard the giant bells of the cathedral pound out their tidings, I could not feel his absence.

That came later, when I received the manuscript of his book *Sabbatical Journey*. At first I received only the pages on which I was mentioned; they astonished and touched me, like letters from beyond the grave. Then I received the whole book, and as I read it I became infuriated. In this chronicle of the last year of his life, one finds all the strains of restlessness—the mad dashes to the airplane, the kaleidoscope of people and places, the promises to himself swiftly broken as he responds to new needs and invitations. And the irony is that I was partly angry with him for having been so nice to me—for having come to the important events in my life, for having responded so quickly when there were so many other demands on his time.

We read most books with a sense of accomplishment as the chapters go by, a pleasurable anticipation as we near the conclusion. In reading *Sabbatical Journey,* I felt instead a sense of foreboding. Every time I turned a page, I realized that I was getting closer not just to the end of the book but to the end of Henri's life. His running commentaries on the past, present, and future—including a passage in which he speculates about what he and I would be talking about in twenty years—are all tinged with poignancy. When I reached the final sentence, the permanence of his death sank in. His voice had fallen silent; his words had ceased.

Yet, even in this final chronicle, Henri offered me a lasting insight. He reminded me that we live our lives as though we were the central characters. Others arrive and depart, but our attention is circumscribed by the boundaries of our own existence. For those who came to know him in person or through his writing, he appeared, offered his words, and then stepped off our stage and onto someone else's. Henri, in a sense, traveled from life to life, from set to set. Now, in the aftermath of his death, we can look together at his journey in its entirety; we can begin to perceive Henri's life as Henri himself experienced it. We can see his tenacious confidence in the love of Christ; his long sojourn as a stranger in strange lands; his virtues and foibles; his marvelous skill at bringing people together and giving them a glimpse of the kingdom; and God's eventual and merciful answer to Henri's plea for a family and a home.

A Sunday school teacher once took her class on a tour of a church that had elaborate stained glass windows. "Can anyone tell me what a saint is?" she asked. One girl raised her hand. "A saint," said the girl laughing, "is someone the light shines through."

Henri would have been appalled to be called a saint. But in the eighteen years I knew him he handed me many pieces of glass and invited me to assemble them. He did this for millions of others, too. Those who loved him are now bringing these bits of glass together, discovering new shapes and images of grace. As we do, we are again touched with surprise—and gratitude—for the gifts that he gave us and the light that shone through.

A Carpenter's Story

JOE CHILD

Joe Child and his wife, Kathy Kelly, came to L'Arche Daybreak from Massachusetts in 1990. Joe was educated as a teacher, owned and managed two funeral homes, and became a woodworker. Today he manages the Daybreak Woodery woodworking shop, a place of employment for several of the community's members. In 1994, Henri confirmed Joe in the Roman Catholic Church.

Not long after my wife, Kathy, and I arrived at Daybreak, she came home with the news that Henri wanted to see me about building a new Eucharist table.

A Eucharist table! My first thought was, "Why is Henri asking me?" And my first worry was, "A Eucharist table is not just another table, but something sacred, and I'm not sure I can do this."

I didn't know Henri very well, so I wasn't in a hurry to talk to him. Also, Henri didn't know me or the kind of work I could do, so I wondered why he'd asked me. Although I had a solid background as a woodworker, my strength came in working from a good set of plans. I did not feel that designing was anywhere near my strong suit. Again, Kathy came home and said Henri really wanted to see me and that I should give him a call.

When Henri and I finally got together, we went down to our chapel, where he said he needed a different type of table from the high, heavy table he had there. When the community gathered for mass, some people sat in chairs around the periphery of the room while others in the center were seated on the floor. Henri said it felt awkward to be standing over so many people on the floor. If I could build a table that would come to about the height of his knees, then he could sit in his chair and everybody could see all the elements of the mass. It would be much more intimate and inclusive. He also said he wanted the table to be easily movable so he could set up the chapel for large or small groups. I knew he liked nice things, but he said very little about how he wanted the table to look. I was struck by Henri's implicit trust in me.

We tried different heights, and finally Henri said that nineteen inches would be perfect. He asked if I could build him his table and when would it be done. I protested that a design was needed first, which would take some time. We finally parted, I promising to get back to him as soon as I had a plan.

I felt a little intimidated about this project. I wasn't then a Catholic. Henri wasn't just another priest, but a theologian with a worldwide reputation. And the community I lived in would use this table to celebrate mass every day.

I thought about the table for a couple of months. I didn't want to make one with four legs because Henri could just go buy a table like that at a store. It had to be out of the ordinary somehow—kind of like Henri was.

One of the great symbols of L'Arche is an ark—Noah's ark—the boat where all are welcomed, the boat that offers shelter in times of need, a place of safety and community for growth and

new life. Somehow I felt that a boat-shaped table would lend itself
to our needs and be appropriate for Daybreak.

When I was living in Massachusetts, our woodworking shop
had created some hourglass pedestals using three-quarter-inch plywood circles stacked and glued. After they were all glued together,
we rounded them out on a slow-turning lathe, leaving edges of
hundreds of layers of plywood. The final shape was achieved with
a disk sander. I began to see a pedestal layered this way and shaped
somewhat like the hull of a sailboat, quite narrow in the midsec-
tion and widening to hold the top of the table, which would be
separate so that it could be lifted off for easy movement or temporary storage.

I was starting to feel more confident that this might work after
all. The only nagging worry was that the stacked laminate displays
I had made in Northampton were round and done on a lathe,
whereas the design I was thinking of for the Eucharist table would
be asymmetrical. Had I thought of every step?

I made two drawings, one a side view and the other an end
view, took them to Henri, and explained the ark theory. He really
liked the symbolism and asked what kind of wood should be used.
I favored cherry because it doesn't need stain to make it beautiful.
Henri was excited and wanted to know when I could start. I wasn't
sure. At the Woodery we had a lot of urgent jobs coming in. I felt
that this project would have to be done in our spare time.

By then it was January. I asked Henri when he wanted the table,
and he said that it would be nice to have it by the beginning of
Lent. I naively agreed that that was possible, and we parted, he
probably more confident in what he was getting than I in knowing
how to build this thing.

I went to Canadian Hardwoods, a small hardwood dealer in
King City from which the Woodery has bought wood off and on

for years. When I told them what I had planned, they said they had some old cherry that was badly warped and, if I wanted it, they would throw it in with my order.

It was, as they'd said, really warped. One piece, about ten feet long, was so warped it started at my waist, bent to the ground, and curved back up to the waist of one of the other men. That's a pretty bad warp by anybody's standards. We took all the cherry they gave us, paid for the rest, and returned to the Woodery to begin milling out the wood. The warped boards were cut into very short pieces so they could be easily flattened. All of these pieces, rejected as unfit to sell, became the base for the table. It seemed so right for our community. People whom society deems worthless, L'Arche recognizes as valuable and, in a way, makes sacred.

John Bloss, one of the core members in the Woodery, was my helper throughout this project. He went with me to pick out the cherry, helped do all the milling and jointing to make the boards

John Bloss with the cherrywood base.

uniform in thickness and size, and helped glue up the hundreds of pieces of wood. Whenever I think of this project, John's face is as clear and present to me as is the shape of the table.

It took much longer than I expected to assemble all of this cherry into what the plans indicated it should look like. Lent had started, and the end of the project was not in sight. Henri would come by the shop often to see how it was going and give encouragement, and he always wanted to know when it would be done and, then, if it would be done for Easter. Sometimes he would bring visitors to see it. He was clearly excited by the emerging design—his curiosity was piqued. We said we would try for Easter. It would be a stretch.

But finally the hull-shaped base was carved and fitted to the tabletop. It looked like a table, yet my eyes were telling me it was not finished. I didn't know what to do to make it look completed.

Providence intervened at this point. At home I received a call from my friend Rob Macks. Rob is a sculptor, and we had done woodworking and whitewater boating together for years. He was driving to Detroit to visit his mother and wanted to stay the night with us. When he came, I showed him the table. He walked around it several times with a raised eyebrow and finally said, "You've built something that is all curves, and the square-cut ends don't accent that. Round off both ends and you'll have it!"

It made wonderful sense. We grabbed a jigsaw, quickly roughed out soft curves on either end of the table, and suddenly I saw what I was looking for.

It took about two more weeks of sanding and lacquering to finish it. We put on fifteen coats of lacquer, sanding it down each time. Even today I know every wave of the grain in the wood. On Saturday at the Easter Vigil service, the table was presented to the community. Henri draped a sheet over it so nobody could see it until everyone had arrived. He was clearly thrilled as he presented it. And it did look beautiful—more beautiful than I'd ever imagined. He asked me to talk about how it was built, where the wood came from, the symbolism, and John's part in it all.

I always remember how intimidated I was when Henri asked me to build our Eucharist table. Somehow, he pulled out of me something I did not know was there. It stretched me to my limits. The final result was not just something built by me but the accumulation of teaching I'd received from various people and many experiences that I had lived over a long period of time. Henri encouraged me to use all of this in a way I had not thought possible.

Now when I sit at mass and look at it, I realize that the table I built for Henri was Henri's gift to me.

The finished altar.

Henri and Daybreak: A Story of Mutual Transformation

MARY BASTEDO

Mary Bastedo was chair of the spiritual life committee at L'Arche Daybreak when Henri arrived in the community. An occupational therapist, she is also a consecrated laywoman, musician, and longtime L'Arche member. Mary is currently working with families who have someone with a disability living at home.

Henri Nouwen's arrival at L'Arche Daybreak in the fall of 1986 raised a few eyebrows. Daybreak was a fairly simple rural community, centered on a hundred acres of farmland just north of Richmond Hill, Ontario. Walking down the dirt laneway, past the pond and the big green barn, we could catch a whiff of the chickens, see John Smeltzer, one of the core members, out on the tractor, and watch the cows in the field and the sheep grazing in the apple or-chard. When I arrived in May 1983, meetings, too, were simple. Monday mornings, the guys from the farm and the woodworking shop and all the assistants, often with children on a few laps, sat around a crowded table to catch up on the news. Tuesdays, the assistants gathered in one of our homes, sitting mostly on the floor, to listen to a spiritual reflection by the community leader and to share what was inspiring to them in their day-to-day life.

In 1984 we built a meeting hall, where we could gather for community meetings, liturgies, Christmas dinner, and the like. It also became the home of a daytime activity program for newer core members (as the people with developmental disabilities are called) who had more challenging needs. Our activities were simple: washing the van, making soup, dancing, singing, swimming at the local pool, horseback riding.

In September 1986, as I was pushing Adam Arnett in his wheelchair to the day program, a big yellow moving van full of Henri's possessions pulled in. Most assistants arrive with a backpack and a few possessions; here was a professor from Harvard arriving with all of this! Hence the raised eyebrows.

Some of us had met Henri during his earlier visit. It was clear that he hardly knew how to make toast and tea, yet he was going to be a house assistant at the New House. Henri had purchased a brand-new car and was driving with his soon-to-be head of house, talking excitedly about how he just wanted to live a normal life. Suddenly they crashed into the car ahead. "This is *not* normal!" the head of house commented. And Henri had to buy another new car.

The man we met at that time was very nervous—not sure whether he'd be able to fit in and insecure in his relationships. Yet he brought the gift of priesthood. Many of us had seen during Henri's first visit his capacity to care for us in a time of crisis. During his weeklong stay, Raymond Batchelor, one of the core members in the New House, was struck by a car as he tried to cross the busy highway in front of Daybreak. Henri was immediately present—to Raymond, to his family, and to the Daybreak community—bringing comfort and leading us in prayer. That experience inspired us to invite him to be our pastor.

It was a new step for us. We had never had a pastor. Various priests, both Anglican and Roman Catholic, had been friends of the community or had lived with us for several months, usually on sabbatical. But our liturgical life was sporadic. And ecumenically we were in a painful place because the lack of agreement among the churches on intercommunion affected our celebration of the Eucharist. The discomfort was leading some members to avoid our community liturgies altogether.

We knew we needed spiritual leadership. Henri, with his broad experience and pastoral sensitivity, seemed to be just the right person to help us. His writing was familiar to many L'Arche assistants. I had been very encouraged by his book *Reaching Out*, which I read during the difficult transition of leaving another L'Arche community. It was clear to me that Henri understood our spirituality, the concept of the wounded healer, the truth that we are all handicapped but that through our brokenness God can be very present.

Henri's way of celebrating liturgy also suited us. We already loved candles and icons, Taizé chants, and low altars draped with colorful cloths and flowers. Henri multiplied those things for us a hundredfold! I remember the first Christmas we celebrated with him in our meeting hall. There were candles everywhere, many of them on the floor. Henri moved excitedly about, his vestments brushing against the flames. Our community leader, who was always a stickler about fire safety, did not have a very prayerful experience that evening!

Celebrating a first communion at a Daybreak liturgy:
Francis Maurice, Henri, and Patrick Egan.

Henri had a gift for seizing the moment—seeing opportunities for celebration and knowing how to mark them liturgically. I was deeply touched by his offer to celebrate a Eucharist of missioning for me when I was sent to be the community leader of L'Arche Stratford, a few hours' drive west of Daybreak, in 1987. He organized the event, with both communities present. I was literally sent by one group and received by the other.

During the six years that I was away from Daybreak, the community encountered some major difficulties. Henri, struggling to respond to the huge relational demands of community life, went into a personal crisis and had to leave for several months. Daybreak faced losing its rural identity and being invaded by bulldozers, noise, and dust as new homes and streets were built all around it. It also experienced major growing pains as the community increased in size and complexity. And it went through a leadership crisis, in which there was conflict and hurt.

In June 1993, when I returned to Daybreak, I found that both Henri and the community had been through a transformation. Nathan Ball had become the community leader. The shared vision and good relationship that had emerged between Henri and Nathan brought stability. It was the first time responsibility for Daybreak's spiritual life had been separated from the role of community leader.

The farm manager's bungalow had become a retreat house, where both Henri and Sue Mosteller lived, with a new wheelchair-accessible chapel in the basement. There was a well-attended daily Eucharist at 8:30 A.M. Once a week it was an Anglican Eucharist, celebrated by Wendy Lywood, an Anglican priest who had come to live in one of the community houses. A new ecumenical harmony had emerged. Non-Catholics were feeling at home. A liturgical dance troupe had been formed. Henri had established a pastoral team of fifteen assistants and core members. He had taught some core members to be altar servers. Some assistants had been mandated to give reflections on the Word, having taken a workshop with Henri. Traditions were developing for Holy Week, always involving the core members in ways that enriched the liturgies.

Several people, both core members and assistants, who had no previous church affiliation, had been baptized or received into local churches. The pastoral team was supervising regular visits to two community members who were terminally ill. One core member had died while I was away. The community had been deeply touched by their experience of caring for him right up until his death. The Bat Mitzvah of Ellen Weinstein, one of the Jewish core members, had led the community into a deeper embrace of its interfaith reality.

This transformation in Daybreak's community life paralleled a personal transformation in Henri. He had grown in inner peace.

When I walked into the chapel in 1993, I knew he had found his place at Daybreak. He was much more secure, more comfortable, more fatherly. He had made that passage, which he describes in *The Return of the Prodigal Son,* to becoming the father. He laughed more easily and full-heartedly. He was more relaxed.

This mutual transformation was the fruit of faithfulness through times of suffering on both sides. Henri's transformation was possible because of the community welcoming and accepting him in his pain, remaining faithful to him when he was away, forgiving him when he disappointed people or kept getting caught in the same old excesses and compulsions. It was the fruit of the community seeing the value and gift of Henri's presence through all the struggles, believing in him, and calling him to continue to grow and put down roots at Daybreak.

The community's transformation was the fruit of Henri's acceptance of individuals where they were on their life journeys: always taking an interest, always encouraging, never rejecting. He had a gift for listening in community meetings as well as in individual counseling. He could summarize and give succinct and insightful feedback. He was able to point out the unity and direction emerging beyond what people actually said, and he helped Daybreak live through its period of struggle by calling people to deeper interiority and prayer.

Today important elements of Henri's vision and practice continue to shape our life together and, I believe, are prophetic not just for Daybreak but for the many communities of L'Arche around the world and for countless other faith communities. Three key qualities of Henri's ministry have been transforming for me.

The first is inclusivity. This is the quality of Henri's ministry that most remains with me. He was ecumenical in the true sense of the word. Henri used a language that not only was inclusive of both men and women but was simple and contemporary, cutting across denominational boundaries and intellectual differences. His liturgical practice was also inclusive: having everyone sit in a circle, welcoming guests, offering the Eucharist to all those who in good conscience felt called to receive it, and blessing those who chose not to receive. Likewise, Henri sensitively welcomed those of other faiths who occasionally visited, and the community began to develop interfaith friendships. He lived his priesthood not as something that excluded others but rather as a way to invite others into participation.

Henri was very attentive to individuals in their personal journeys, encouraging them in their struggles. He could raise questions without being judgmental. He was able to live with the gray. This quality challenged me. As the community leader of a small community, I had been accustomed to making clear-cut decisions. I was more black-and-white about what was acceptable in community life. Yet I saw the fruitfulness of Henri's approach, saw people finding and growing in faith and making commitments in the light of faith. I saw the vitality of a community that was able to embrace diversity and encourage creativity. I was challenged to stretch my boundaries and to learn to live with the gray.

Another key element of Henri's spirituality was intimacy. Henri always struggled with intimacy: yet he was able to achieve it, especially in his capacity to move in close to those who were suffering. We witnessed this with Raymond and his family after the car accident and we saw it repeatedly. Henri taught the community a lot about compassionate presence to those who are suffering and, especially, to those who are dying. All that we learned was preparation for Henri's own death, when we held a wake and an all-night vigil and organized a three-hour funeral celebration.

A third aspect of Henri's ministry that has influenced me is the way he spoke inspirationally about the gift that the poor or marginal person can carry for the rest of us—the gift of L'Arche. For years before Henri arrived, Sue Mosteller had been saying, "L'Arche is about much more than living in a home with people who have a disability." Henri's coming to Daybreak helped us find the words to express what L'Arche is and share it with a much wider circle. Today we speak of L'Arche as a school of the heart, where we learn the values of hospitality, compassion, forgiveness, and mutual relationship; a place where we discover that the apparently poor person has much to give to others; a place where we get in touch with our own poverty and limits and find God's presence in our weakness; a place where we learn to know who God is as a lover and friend.

One of the dangers in L'Arche is isolation. Assistants can be taken up by the challenges of everyday life in the homes and work programs. Henri helped us to overcome this insularity. His books and speaking engagements made L'Arche better known in North America. His celebration of Sunday mass in our local parish high-

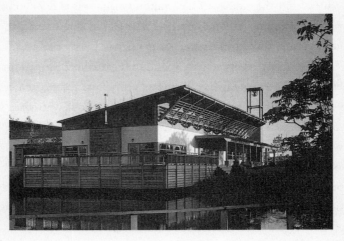

The new Dayspring building viewed from across the Daybreak pond.

lighted our presence in Richmond Hill. His retreats for leaders of various denominations made us visible in the Toronto area. It was always striking to see visitors come to Daybreak to be with Henri but in the end be most touched by and ministered to in sharing a meal in one of the Daybreak homes and getting to know some of the core members.

Henri helped us have confidence that we do have something to say to the world around us. The new Dayspring chapel, which was Henri's dream and for which he raised most of the funds, was completed in January 1999. It has become a place where community members are being empowered to share about their lives and thus enable many more people to experience our spirituality. Every week high school students come for retreat days, and many people from Toronto and afar participate in periodic days of reflection offered by the community. In the fall of 1998, Daybreak asked me to explore a ministry to families who have a child with a disability living at home. Several of these families now come to our weekly community worship. Faith and Light support groups for persons who have disabilities, their families, and young volunteers have also sprung from this work.

It is with deep gratitude that I reflect on Henri Nouwen's life and its impact on L'Arche Daybreak. Daybreak helped Henri to make a passage of personal growth and to discover a great fruitfulness in the last ten years of his life. Henri helped Daybreak to make a passage into spiritual maturity and a dynamic sense of mission. This mutual transformation created a legacy to be shared, a treasure for which we are now taking responsibility.

After Adam Died

MICHAEL ARNETT

Michael Arnett has lived at L'Arche Daybreak since 1978. Adam, his brother, joined him there in 1985. When Adam died in February 1996, just seven months before Henri died, Michael turned to Henri, his friend and pastor, for comfort. Michael asked Beth Porter to write down his recollections for this contribution. He spoke slowly, often pausing to find his words.

After Adam died, me did go right over to Father Henri's place, Dayspring. He talk to me about Adam. Me say to him, "I don't know why Adam was like that—dead. . . . How come people die?"

Father Henri says to me—what stays in my head—Father Henri says, "My Father is up in heaven and my brother is up in heaven."

I loved Adam this much. *(Michael spreads his arms wide.)*

Father Henri gave me a big hug. I cried . . . I hugged Father Henri . . . I got my voice on a tape with Henri . . . talking about Adam, on the tape.

Michael Arnett with his brother, Adam.

Me did go in that car—Father Henri's car. Father Henri did give me that big cross. He give me books . . . car books . . . horse books.

Father Henri say to me, "You want to cry? You come over to my house." Father Henri missed Adam too.

When Father Henri died I felt sad. . . . My heart was broken.

Father Henri *is* with Adam . . . in heaven, now . . . with God.

Sometimes I do sit on Adam's bench. Right by Daybreak pond. Think about Adam. Think about Henri.

ON LIVING THE
RESURRECTED LIFE

As a community of people conscious of our disabilities, we are held together not so much by the Word as by the body. Although we use many words and there is a lot of "talk" among us, it is the weak bodies of our core members that create community. We wash, shave, comb, dress, clean, feed, and hold the bodies of those who are entrusted to us and thus build a communal body. As we claim our faith in the resurrection of the body, we come to see that the resurrection is not simply an event after death but a reality of everyday life. Our care for the body calls us to unity beyond organization, to intimacy beyond eroticism, and to integrity beyond psychological wholeness.

Unity, intimacy, and integrity are the three spiritual qualities of the resurrected life. We are called to break through the boundaries of nationality, race, sexual orientation, age, and mental capacities and create a unity of love that allows the weakest among us to live well. We are called to go far beyond the places of lust, sexual need, and desire for physical union to a spiritual intimacy that involves body, mind, and heart. And we are called to let go of old ways of feeling good about ourselves and reach out to a new integration of the many facets of our humanity. These calls are calls to the resurrection. Caring for the body is preparing the body for the final resurrection while anticipating it in our daily lives through spiritual unity, intimacy, and integrity.

—*Sabbatical Journey*

A New Way
to Live

ANDREW KENNEDY

Andrew Kennedy knew Henri as his spiritual mentor. Andrew and his wife, Andrea, became friends of L'Arche Daybreak, and Andrew served on the community's board of directors. They now live with their children, George and Beatrice, in London, England, where Andrea is a children's television producer and Andrew is working at a large international bank.

To describe my friendship with Henri, I first need to write briefly about my brother, Michael. For it was through Michael that I met Henri. In the late 1980s, Michael began to suffer from progressively worse bouts of mental anguish. My family, in their search for answers, reached out to a number of psychiatric specialists and mental health practitioners. Because no two doctors could agree on a diagnosis, Michael and my family descended into the hopeless and horrific world of psychiatric wards, tranquilizers, and a medical system that seemed largely indifferent to our needs. My parents lived in Toronto and had heard of Henri. They were aware that he was part of a L'Arche community just north of the city and that, as well as being a priest, he had trained in psychology and psychiatry. In their search for help, they tried contacting Henri through a mutual friend to see if he would possibly meet with my brother.

Within a couple of days my parents got word that he would like to see Michael, and a meeting was arranged for the following week. Henri's immediate and passionate response to the request from my parents—people he had never met—caught us all a bit off guard at the time, but as I came to know him better, he always amazed me with his willingness to enter into the lives of others, often complete strangers.

Henri and Michael began to develop quite a close friendship. Henri never spoke about the details of their meetings, but he did share with us what he perceived as Michael's deep spiritual angst and struggle living in the world. However, although Henri's friendship and counseling seemed to be a tremendous comfort to him, Michael continued to descend into a very dark place, and he took his own life on March 5, 1992.

Immediately upon hearing of Michael's death, Henri rushed down to my parents' house with Bill Van Buren. I had just returned home from university to be with my family, and it was the first time I met Henri. Although my memories of that time still seem dreamlike, I clearly remember Henri gathering us in a small circle and talking and praying with us. I also remember, even in such tragic circumstances, finding something comic and tremendously endearing about Henri as he spoke to us so intensely with his strong, at times incomprehensible, Dutch accent; his long, gangly legs crossed one over the other with one foot tucked under the other calf as though tangled in a knot; and his huge, expressive, and somewhat clumsy hands wildly gesticulating as if they were having a separate conversation with us. Another thing that struck me was the way he consumed me when I spoke.

The intensity of his focus was so strong, it was as though nothing else in the world existed for him during a conversation. It was also quite remarkable to see his courage and willingness to enter directly into the pain of our loss and stand beside us and share our mourning.

Henri delivered the homily at Michael's memorial service. It was powerful and challenging. He spoke about Michael's creativity, deep love, and profound sensibility. He also spoke about the forces of darkness and rejection that raged within him. And he bluntly told how Michael had lost the battle for life—how he had died alone, feeling useless and a burden to his family and friends, not worthy of any attention or care. He spoke about how all of us who had loved Michael and witnessed his suffering also lost the battle for life. He drew parallels to Jesus' death on the cross, alone, rejected, and misunderstood, and stated that Jesus had lost the battle, too. And in the same way that Jesus' friends experienced complete failure in his death, we felt as though all hope had been lost in Michael's death. But it was only in this tremendous loss and immense pain that we would be able to come to know something about love that we would never have come to know without Michael. And through this knowledge, each of us would discover a new freedom to love.

When Henri had finished, there was silence. Some people were shocked and offended by his forceful words. But most were profoundly touched by his raw, truthful message that avoided easy answers. His sermon was like his life—he rolled up his sleeves and threw himself right into the heart of the matter. He didn't have any simple, clichéd answers. Instead, he paid tribute to the anguish we all felt and pointed to it as the place where our hearts must live to be reborn and where our shared humanity is discovered. It was a message of pain and loss but also one of hope and rebirth.

The way Henri threw himself into my family's life attests to his enormous willingness to enter into the core of our shared human experience. He never shied away from embracing the complication of it all. For Henri knew that at the very center of our pain and the vulnerability that accompanied it lay a transcendent truth, which, if properly nourished, would lead directly to a better understanding of the wounded heart of God.

Almost two years passed before I saw Henri again. I was busy finishing law school, newly married, and, quite frankly, just wanted to shut down and close out the pain. The only memento of Michael I carried with me was a copy of his obituary. I kept it in my wallet but rarely looked at it since it would always bring back a flood of confused pain. It became my secret talisman, hidden but always present to ward off my evil spirits. So, I worked hard during my articling year at a law firm, kept occupied with a number of hobbies, played music with friends, and generally did whatever I could to stay busy and not think too much.

At the end of that very hectic year, I had the summer off. I had been looking forward to a break and hoped to just relax. I had been working sixty- to eighty-hour weeks in Toronto, and Andrea, my wife, was living and working in Ottawa at the time, so I was regularly making the four-and-a-half-hour drive from Toronto to see her on weekends. One of my brothers had just returned from a year as an assistant at a L'Arche community in France, and he had brought home tapes of a retreat led by Jean Vanier. I decided to listen to some of these while making the weekly trek to Ottawa. Part of the tapes spoke of our society's obsession with strength and competitiveness in order to guard our hearts from being vulnerable. Yet how deeply wounded we all are, especially those who seek to deny it. Jean spoke to me with such simplicity and power that I found myself sobbing uncontrollably and had to pull off the northern Ontario highway.

The following week or so, my life took a nosedive. All my carefully constructed walls, fences, dikes, and dams began to crack. I had never really faced the wounds of my brother's death, my marriage was in tatters as we maintained the facade of weekend visits, and in my drive to shut out all the hurt, insecurity, and uncertainty of my troubles, I began to realize that I had lost myself.

After listening to Jean's tapes, I hungered for someone who would help me recover and rebuild a spiritual foundation for my life. It became obvious that I needed to speak with a spiritual counselor, but I had no idea how to go about finding one. I decided to ask Henri who he could recommend. I was very apprehensive about writing to him since we had met only twice some time ago and I was certain he would have far more pressing matters to deal with. Nonetheless, I plucked up the courage, briefly explained my circumstances, and asked whether he could suggest a spiritual counselor in the Ottawa area.

Within about four days, I received a note the size of a postcard with a photograph of lilies on its reverse. Henri wrote to say that he would be in Ottawa for a day the following week and could we meet then? I was to call to set up a time.

As it turned out, Henri was flying to Ottawa to deliver a homily at the funeral of a former member of Parliament and was to attend a reception at Parliament afterwards. It was agreed that I should seek him out at the reception, and we would try to sneak off to talk for a few moments.

I arrived at the appointed time but needed to convince the parliamentary guards that I was there to meet a priest at a reception hosted by the Speaker of the House. I finally made it through and waded into a hall where three or four hundred people were enjoying tea, coffee, and desserts. I spotted Henri halfway down the hall. He was speaking to a small group of admirers. His gray flannels, blue button-down shirt, tweed jacket, and tie all made him look the part of the Harvard academic. In one hand he held a coffee and in the other some dessert. He was trying to speak, drink, and eat all at the same time while wildly gesturing with those massive hands. I could tell that many of his listeners could not exactly follow his torrent of Dutch-thick English, but no one seemed to mind one bit. And Henri was clearly enjoying himself.

I introduced myself, and he embraced me as though we were old friends. He introduced me to his newest circle of acquaintances, continued chatting, and eventually suggested we find somewhere quiet to talk.

We ended up meeting in the office of the Speaker of the House. So there I was, sitting by a large fireplace in an enormous oak-paneled room and baring my deepest soul to this most peculiar Dutch priest.

We spoke for about an hour. At the end, Henri asked if we could pray together. He prayed a beautiful prayer about God's continuous desire for each of us to learn to love and forgive ourselves and to know how deeply we are beloved of God. He also prayed for Michael and prayed that Michael would watch over me as I traveled the road to healing. As we were leaving, I asked Henri if he could recommend anyone as a spiritual adviser, and, with a wry grin, he suggested himself.

So began our relatively short but strong friendship, which started in the same way that many of Henri's friendships began: a cry for help to which he immediately responded with a simple, loving embrace.

I began traveling to Daybreak once, sometimes twice a week to meet with Henri. We would usually talk for an hour or so. My mind was always bursting with questions. He had an uncanny ability to express often complex thoughts in simple, communicable ways. We would talk about how to develop a sense of identity rooted in God as opposed to the world, how to juggle a demanding career with a contemplative spirituality, how our wounds and shortcomings can transform us and lead to a deeper compassion for others, and, of course, we spoke a lot about Michael.

Although I did not know it at the time, the next few months would literally change the way Andrea and I lived. But it all happened slowly, a step at a time.

From the very start, Henri encouraged me to get to know the Daybreak community. So I spent many happy hours sharing meals, meeting core members and assistants, and attending the community's frequent services and celebrations. To be honest, at first I was not that interested in meeting these new people and participating in the constant stream of community events. I only really wanted to spend time with Henri. But as time passed, I came to understand and appreciate the community and the integral part it played in Henri's own life, and I began to cherish my time there. This was also Henri's way of saying that if I wanted to know him and, more important, deepen my understanding of God's presence in my life, I would have to know Daybreak. For Daybreak was where Henri's spirituality lived and breathed. Although he never lost his restless need to travel, meet new friends, and gain new insights, Daybreak was the home he always returned to for comfort, solace, and fellowship.

Henri and Andrea quickly became friends, too. They first met at an animated lunch at the Green House with core members and assistants. Following a stroll through the community, we ended up at the Daybreak bookshop, which unfortunately was closed. Henri rummaged through his pocket, pulled out a key, and proceeded to load us up with books, tapes, pictures, and other mementos. There was so much we could barely carry it all. When we asked whether he should contact someone to explain why all these things were missing, he sheepishly laughed and admitted he was certain to get into trouble for it but not to worry.

Andrea and I both recall the many happy hours we shared in Henri's room talking, surrounded by his beautiful icons, books, a cassette player, paintings, and photographs. His room showed Henri's simple but elegant taste. He was also able to both live in the lofty world of ideas and holiness and talk about contemporary issues or the latest films and best-selling books. For Henri, every facet of life seemed to present an opportunity to see God.

Throughout the fall and winter of 1994–95, Andrea often joined me for my meetings with Henri and my journeys to Daybreak. In early 1995 we discussed with Henri how the two of us could together make a more formal commitment to the church and also to Daybreak as a community. Andrea had been raised a Catholic but had never been confirmed, and I had been baptized and confirmed as an Anglican. So for the lingering weeks of that winter through to the thawed, renewing days of spring, Andrea and I walked the road to Easter with Henri. We continued our weekly meetings and used the time to explore the role of the church in our lives, the meaning of redemption and incarnation, and the mystical implications of a transcendent God present not only in our own lives but also in the lives of those around us.

On the Saturday evening before Easter, core members, Daybreak assistants, and friends, family, and others from far and wide gathered in the old Dayspring chapel for the vigil. It was a beautiful service full of pregnant, waiting hope. The chapel, lit only by candles, was somber and still as we heard about the promise of new life. Henri confirmed Andrea, and I was received into the Roman Catholic Church. At the close of the service, he gave us a beautiful, inscribed copy of a Rembrandt etching—*Christ Healing the Sick.*

We had initially been quite hesitant about "getting religious," but as we continued to meet with Henri and came to know the Daybreak community, it became apparent that genuine faith and belief rarely arise through eureka-like revelations but instead occur by means of a slow, gradual turning of our hearts. And Henri understood that the religious life is not about being some "holy" person; instead it is about planting seeds, nourishing the seedlings to root, and fostering a dialogue about the spiritual life and one's own spiritual issues that can be sustained through a lifetime.

Turning religious scared us because we thought it would mean so many difficult things—such as forsaking material comforts and pleasures and associating only with like-minded "Christians"—attributes that in our minds were narrowing and uncomfortable. Henri, however, helped open our eyes to a whole world of intellectual and spiritual living that was so freeing and broadening that, after several years, Andrea and I felt as though we were different people. We had a different marriage to show for it, our friendships with others deepened, our priorities started to shift, and I like to think we embarked on a more mindful, intentional way of living.

Our new perspectives began to infuse all the little, private, ordinary events of everyday life. No longer could we share a meal with friends without remembering Henri teaching us about the meaning of communion. And it got harder and harder to complain about our lives without first reminding ourselves of all their simple, self-evident abundance. We became mindful of the importance of acceptance, respect, and love as cornerstones for our marriage. We also learned to acknowledge and encourage each other's aspirations and to ground our commitment to each other in a faith that could weather the occasional storm.

As I recall this time, I am filled with vivid, fond memories. I had an insatiable hunger to learn about this new world I was discovering. And Daybreak—always a stimulating environment—was especially fascinating for me. On weekends the house where Henri lived was constantly full of visitors. Andrea and I spent many happy evenings sharing a glass of wine or a meal with an extraordinary variety of people: peace activists who had worked with the Berrigan brothers, Wall Street lawyers, Croatian nuns, South American priests, Ivy League academics, U.S. Air Force chaplains, AIDS activists, poets, writers, sculptors, and hospice workers, to name but a few. The common thread we all shared was a deep affection for Henri and how he had, in individual ways, quietly changed our lives.

After my years of grieving, Henri also brought me to a place of peace around Michael's death. I began to see my brother's life within a larger context and became grateful for all that I had learned from him. Out of the pain and suffering I had experienced grew a deeper appreciation of the fragility and beauty of life, which I am certain would not have been possible without Michael. And out of it I realized the crucial importance of honoring the struggles in our own lives and the lives of those around us. In every moment lies an opportunity to affirm, support, love, and be thankful or to hide, hurt, run, and resent. The choice is ours. So when Henri entered my life, I felt as though Michael had somehow prepared me to be grateful for the gift of Henri's guidance, kindness, and presence.

Of course, life during this time was not all easy. We had the usual ups and downs. But Henri was always there as a source of comfort and wisdom, whether the problem was career crisis, family troubles, religious questions, or just the need for someone to talk to. He delighted in Andrea's first pregnancy and then shared our grief when she miscarried. He would send us short notes with copies of his newest books and call us occasionally to say hello, but generally life moved on and we all gradually got busier with other things. In September 1995, Henri began a one-year sabbatical away from Daybreak. I saw him just before he left and he seemed very, very tired. I hoped and prayed the break would be good for him.

The year of his sabbatical I became a member of the board of directors of Daybreak. We spent a lot of time discussing the community's future, and we all recognized the great void caused by Henri's absence as well as our overdependence on him. We began to focus on developing the other resources and riches in the community. In retrospect it's clear that Henri's sabbatical was a year of preparation for the community. Henri's absence made us all aware of how maturity—whether as a community or as individuals—entails standing with confidence and not relying on any single person, no matter how extraordinary, to the exclusion of others.

I can clearly remember the day in September 1996 when we received the call telling us Henri had died. Andrea and I were at my parents' cottage. She was about five months pregnant with our son, George. The news of Henri's death took the wind right out of us. We had known about his heart attack but were assured that he would be fine. Andrea sat at the dining room table overlooking a calm, autumnal lake and just sobbed and sobbed. How could this remarkable, gregarious, and generous man be dead? It wasn't possible. We'd assumed that we still had so many years of deepening friendship ahead of us; there were so many unfinished conversations. Henri was supposed to christen our baby, to be there when we needed him. I sat in stunned silence for a long time, holding Andrea's hand as she continued to cry, and together we succumbed to a deep, deep feeling of emptiness.

Daybreak held a wake for Henri a few days after his death. The entire community together with some of Henri's closest friends gathered to mourn the loss of this dear friend. It was a moving service, and I remember thinking a lot about Henri's presence in my life and the lives of those around me, and how much he had meant to us all. I also thought about how we, as individuals and as a community, had spent the year of his sabbatical learning to lessen our reliance on him so that we could stand on our own feet while honoring all that he had shown us.

People began to file past the open casket, and I noticed that many of the core members were placing personal keepsakes inside. I struggled to imagine what I could leave with Henri that could in any way express my profound gratitude for all he had done for me. Suddenly it dawned on me. As I wound my way to the front of the line, I pulled out my wallet and dug out a faded, worn obituary notice. I kneeled down, thanked God from the depths of my soul for Henri's life, placed the notice in the casket, and moved on.

Although Henri helped release me from the suffering of Michael's death, Michael, in turn, helped me fully appreciate the gift of Henri's friendship in my life. When Michael died, I had been tortured by remorse and regret concerning the things I did not say to him, the times I did not tell him how much I loved him. And I spent years wondering whether I could have done something to help him before his death. But through Henri I learned to forgive myself for these shortcomings, and in forgiving I was able to free myself from my anguish. I was also able to say thank you to Henri in a way that was impossible before because it was only through Michael that I had come to know the great gift another person can be to one's own life.

To this day it is difficult to express how much Andrea and I miss Henri. How often I wish I could speak to him—not so much anymore for advice or guidance but simply as a treasured friend. I wish we could occasionally share a bottle of wine, that he could meet our children, that he could visit us from time to time in London. Rare is the day that passes when I don't think of him. But the same is true of Michael; in a way they have both become my patron saints. For Michael taught me the meaning of pain and forgiveness, and Henri taught me the meaning of rebirth, new life, and the redemptive power of love. Though it may sound strange to some, I talk with Michael and Henri regularly and ask them to watch over me, my little family, and those we love. I also ask them to keep me on the right track, to help me live a life of honesty, integrity, and courage, not to be afraid of pain and vulnerability, and always to bear in mind the life-giving lessons each of them taught me.

Collision and Paradox

BART AND PATRICIA GAVIGAN

Bart and Patricia Gavigan, filmmakers, writers, and lecturers, are the founders of South Park Community Trust, a British charity. Henri frequently stayed and wrote at Brook Place, their Christian ecumenical center. Their relationship with Henri had many dimensions: friendship, pastoral care, shared ministry, family and community life, and writing collaboration.

In our home there is a crumpled napkin from an Italian restaurant. Scribbled on one side is a crude drawing that looks like the work of a child. In actual fact, its creator was our friend Henri Nouwen.

In the middle of one of our whistle-stop visits to Daybreak, Henri had whooshed us to downtown Toronto to see a new Canadian film, *Jesus of Montreal.* It was a typical Henri move—spontaneous, flexible, and doubtless fueled in part by his nearly permanent craving for stimulation. Henri somehow always managed to have room for other choices. Sometimes he'd set aside densely packed schedules in Rotterdam to fly to London so that we could spend even a few hours together. Once he insisted on taking time out from a grueling film shoot to shop for a toy for our son Gabriel—his godson. Henri had an immense desire to know and participate in what was going on in the world. He loved drama, whether it was a full-blown musical like *Blood Brothers* in London's West End, or T. S. Eliot's *Murder in the Cathedral* in a derelict church in the East End, or the latest subtitled movie from Europe. All were arenas for passion, engagement, and the exploration of humanity.

Jesus of Montreal was an exciting choice. It had us arguing and discussing long into the night over pasta and a bottle of wine. And somewhere in the midst of this animated dialogue Henri whipped out a pen, grabbed his napkin, and scribbled furiously. The dark squiggles, he declared, were the waves of a storm-tossed ocean: our pressurized, stressed lives. Yet far below these churning waves, he demonstrated with huge gesticulation, there is stillness and silence in the murky blackness of the ocean floor. And true peace, Christ's peace, is reached only by plunging down, under the crashing waves of crises that beset our daily lives, to find that eternal peace that is always there, available to us, no matter what is happening on the surface.

Pasta, wine, and passionate theological discussion. Such collision was a staple of Henri's life. Sometimes the results were comic—collision is at the core of all comedy—and sometimes they were intensely moving.

In his address at our wedding, Henri delighted in raising a few eyebrows with a typical stream of paradoxes: "In a marriage what is most hidden becomes most visible; what is most intimate becomes most shared; what is most personal becomes most universal. . . . You sitting here today take on a very special responsibility to care for this couple, because marriage is a very fragile reality. It needs love and support. And it needs *critical* love and support. That is what the Christian community is about. You are not only invited to say nice things to them but to be *critically* present in their life!"

On another occasion Henri was at our ministry center struggling with acute inner turmoil. One morning we had shared a particularly intense pastoral session. Shortly after the session ended we hurried to our home to prepare for a midday house mass. Clearly Henri was suffering inwardly. Yet he threw himself wholeheartedly into the preparations, concentrating on each detail minutely and painstakingly—the candles, the flowers, the readings, the vestments from Guatemala. And the pervading spirit was not escape or denial, but focus. Henri experienced the Eucharist not as an interruption of life but as life itself. It was where he became most truly himself—relaxed, hospitable, fully present. It was a place of creativity and spontaneity, not of rigidity or stifling hierarchy. He loved to bring together both old and new elements: tradition and contemporary expression were neither mutually exclusive nor sparring enemies. His emphasis was on festivity and celebration, on giving, on creating an atmosphere, on the organic.

In fact, exactly the same spirit informed our first meeting in his home at Harvard, a half-hour visit expanded into four or five hours. Only here it was cheese and biscuits instead of unleavened bread, Dutch beer instead of wine.

Henri's whole life was made up of such paradoxes. He loved life intensely. He loved dialogue, discussion, exploration, celebration. He loved analyzing a circus performance, a new cutting-edge tome on theology, a novel or a poem, or whatever book he himself was currently writing.

Yet his life was also deeply marred by the scars of inner deprivation. Henri lived on the edge of an emotional abyss—like a man whose beautiful camper van sits perched just a few feet from the cliff face of a deep quarry. He was generous, but he often acknowledged that his natural inclination was to keep score—counting the times he gave but was not given to, the times he paid but was not paid for.

He had a wonderful, wry sense of humor and an ability to be objective about things that were deeply subjective. Once when we asked him why he had left a pastoral situation where he had been convalescing, his eyes twinkled and he said simply: "They liked me better sick!" Yet, he could also be a mean-spirited grump, a gloomy curmudgeon. The good thing was, these moods rarely lasted for long.

Paradox existed even in his physical being. Henri preached urgently and often the central Christian truth of the incarnation, yet he himself was spectacularly ill at ease in his body. You had only to watch the way he walked or glance at those bitten-to-the-quick fingernails to recognize the inner battle. In Henri's life abundance and deprivation were side by side. Celebration's brightness flowered on the edge of self-destructive darkness; language itself was peppered with oxymorons like "wounded healer" and "creative despair."

Once, after he had given the keynote address to a packed audience of fifteen thousand at the National Catholic Education Convention in Toronto, we sat hunched in a small car in the bowels of the underground garage. Henri wanted a critique of his talk and then of his writing. Above all he wanted to discuss what his next book should be. As a writer he felt as if he were at a crucial crossroads. He wanted his next book to be on the flying trapeze. He wanted the circus story to make the crossover to a secular audience in a way he had never before attempted. He felt it was the most important thing he would ever write. And we encouraged him to go for it. In his own words, to try "a triple" (somersault) and trust the catcher!

But the years passed and the trapeze book never got written. Several times he came to stay at Brook Place laden with research on every aspect of the subject and lugging a huge suitcase crammed with stunning blow-up photographs of the Flying Rodleighs' trapeze act. Yet each time when he left, it was not with a completed circus manuscript. He had written a different book instead.

For Henri the heroic task of spiritual beings trying to live embodied lives was at the very core of theology. He understood that it is not simply suffering that destroys human beings but rather their failure to know that they are chosen, blessed, and loved from all eternity by their Creator. He experienced in his own spirit that the suffering that flows from meaninglessness and being alone is what finally cripples and destroys us.

His life was so enormously fruitful precisely because it embraced this daily struggle. It was hand-to-hand combat with that "absurd life" that Henri himself cataloged with deadly accuracy in his many books: that frenetic world where the urgent eclipses the essential, where being busy and being lonely often coincide, where the house of fear is routinely preferred to the house of love, where we are filled but unfulfilled, physically satiated yet emotionally and spiritually hollow. For not only was incarnation at the heart of all his communication but it was the goal of all his exploration. His dialogue with the world was inspired by a profound theological question: What does it mean to be fully human?

Henri often found himself incarcerated in the house of fear. He often wondered if he would die abandoned. "Will any of my friends come to my funeral?" was a genuine concern for him. In a nutshell, Henri Nouwen, like all of us, taught best what he needed to learn most. And that is why so many find their own struggles and choices in his books, why so many say, "This is my story too!"

Our final memory of Henri is—as ever—collision and paradox.

Yes, his friends did come to his funeral—hundreds of them. And many others, too, who had never met him except in the pages of his books. People like the lonely, divorced, older woman from Amsterdam who squeezed herself into the pew next to us, clutching the newspaper's death notice, tears brimming her eyes; or the lawyer who said brokenly, "I never knew him but I feel as if I have lost my best friend."

Afterwards, when the media cameras had been packed away, Henri's comrades from L'Arche raided the banks of sunflowers around his coffin. Singing and rejoicing, they escorted Henri to the street where the hearse waited. We shall never forget the faces of the passersby across the street staring at the spectacle. Finally one old man blurted out, "This is a *church*?"

His question might well have been "How can such life, such hope, such vigor, such rejoicing, flow out of a church?" Henri would have loved it!

The Reality
Principle

LISA CATALDO

Lisa Cataldo is a doctoral candidate in psychology and religion at Union Theological Seminary in New York City. She also teaches religion in a boys' high school. Lisa continues to stay in touch with her L'Arche Daybreak friends, especially Tracy Westerby, with whom she lived at the Corner House in the summers of 1995 and 1996. Henri was Lisa's spiritual director.

I had just quit my job as a Park Avenue banker when I encountered Henri for the first time. While the corporate life had its rewards, it no longer served me emotionally or spiritually. I was seeking a new path and, through the study of Eastern spirituality, had recently found my way back into the church. I was considering studying for the Episcopal priesthood but struggled with my attachment to the Roman Catholic Church of my upbringing. An Episcopal priest friend recommended that I attend the lecture his old friend Henri Nouwen was giving soon. All I knew about Henri was his book *With Open Hands*, which my friend's wife had given me a few days before. If I had known where the encounter with this intense Dutch priest would lead me, I might have run away. Luckily, I did not.

From the moment I heard Henri speak I was infatuated. I don't mean in a romantic way, but in the way a spiritual seeker in the throes of a conversion is infatuated by the guru. There he was, in the grand chancel of St. Bartholomew's Church in New York City, passionately challenging the audience of eight hundred to move from "greed to gratitude" in that throaty, gurgling Dutch accent, gesticulating wildly, running back and forth along the center aisle. I wondered how he could run up and down the steps without looking, and without tripping. I participated delightedly when Henri stopped in the middle of his talk (it seemed in the middle of a sentence) and teased us into singing with him.

He held the audience as much with his erratic, generous movements as with his words. We all listened very hard to understand Henri, especially when he used words like *gratitude* (this sounded like some combination of water crashing into rocks, gravel spilling down a slate board, and the speech of someone with a very sore throat). He wooed us, he wowed us, and in his charming way he won us over.

Henri had brought along Carl MacMillan and Greg Lannan from the Daybreak community. They each said a few words. Greg, a core member, told us of his difficult life in an institution before he came to live at Daybreak, and he eloquently described the satisfaction he now enjoyed as a contributing member of a community. Carl and Greg interacted with Henri as close friends, certainly without any sense of being starstruck. This amazed me. How did one become so familiar with a "great man" like Henri Nouwen?

Henri emphasized that it was from the core members at Daybreak that he had learned most of what he knew about living the spiritual life. While I didn't doubt his experience, I was sure that it was Henri himself I wanted for my teacher. This is *someone*, I thought. I felt a deep need to meet this man, and to hear what he might have to say about my spiritual journey.

I was invited to a dinner party given to honor Henri. By chance I rode up the elevator with Henri, Carl, and Greg, and briefly introduced myself. Henri was decidedly preoccupied with whether Carl had remembered to bring the supplies for the mass Henri was to say before dinner, and he seemed completely uninterested in me. Then, during the evening, my priest friend and his wife were so keen on my meeting Henri that I was introduced to him four separate times by different people. Each time Henri said, "Yes, I've *met* Lisa." We did get to spend some time talking, and I glimpsed the depth of Henri's understanding and empathy. Although we had known each other for only a few minutes, he seemed able to perceive the heart of my questions about my vocation and the church, and he was present to me in a way that made me feel recognized and greatly valued.

During the evening Greg invited me to visit the Daybreak community, and soon after I took him up on his invitation. I booked myself into the Dayspring for a nine-day retreat, ready to learn "at the feet" of Henri. My room was the small one next to Henri's, and I anticipated all the quality time I would get to spend with my new teacher. It is a great understatement to say that the visit didn't turn out like I'd planned, and it is no exaggeration to say that it changed my life forever.

My acquaintance with Henri during my first retreat at Daybreak both confirmed and confounded my image of him. His energy was of an intensity I had never encountered, and he often nearly bowled me over as he raced from one activity or meeting to another. Several people from the community would gather at 6:30 in the morning for meditation before breakfast. Being a Yoga teacher and faithful meditator, I looked forward to spending this time in prayer with Henri and the others. I was sure that this great man of prayer would teach me much about stillness and contemplation. How wrong I was! Throughout the meditation hour he adjusted his posture, fidgeted, and generally emitted restlessness. It was clear that stillness was *not* something I would learn from Henri.

After meditation Henri orchestrated breakfast for those in the Dayspring. This undertaking, too, was a study in hyperactivity as he sliced bread, made coffee, and set the table. I had never imagined anyone could move so fast so early in the morning. Once I had to duck for cover as Henri made a point about something, forgetting in his dramatic gesturing that the bread knife was still in his hand.

One morning as we were preparing breakfast I set my fruit on the plate opposite Henri's in the hope that I would be able to talk to him over the meal. A few moments later, as Henri rushed around finishing the preparations, he looked at the table and said, "Whose is this?" pointing to the place I had set for myself. Before I could answer he moved my plate to the other corner of the table, replacing it with the plate of his friend Jutta Ayer, who was visiting from Boston. The abruptness and carelessness of his action astounded and wounded me. Was I somehow unwanted or unworthy? Along with being hurt, I was *mad*. What was he thinking?

This episode was deeply revealing, not only of Henri but also of myself. Henri had done something which exposed me to myself. I recognized my hero worship for what it was. I had constructed a Henri in my mind who was the "perfected" spiritual master, not a human being who could make a thoughtless mistake. I realized in a way I hadn't before my ability to idealize people, especially men whom I thought of as authority figures. It was a rude awakening but an important one. And this incident provided a good foundation for the spiritual direction we would soon undertake together.

As a spiritual director Henri showed none of the flightiness or thoughtlessness that sometimes characterized his interaction with the world. One on one, Henri was attentive and insightful to a degree that I have never encountered in another person. I spent many hours with him attempting to discern what God had in mind for me. Our early meetings were punctuated by my anger about the Roman Catholic Church and its treatment of women. I agonized over theological and doctrinal questions. What I wanted was clarity, definitions, black-and-white boundaries. I soon came to learn that this all-or-nothing approach was cut from the same cloth as my idealization of Henri.

Henri never took offense at my often aggressive and unforgiving questions. "How is it," I asked, "that you, a Catholic priest, give communion to Protestants, even though it is against the rules of the church?" Or, "How can the teaching of one denomination be definitive? It is clear that the Catholic Church's policies regarding women are unfair and do not honor the Gospel—how do you explain that?"

Henri's responses displayed his keen perception of my state of mind and level of understanding as well as my need to find a listening ear for my hurts. He gently affirmed my experience while inviting me to understand things in a less rigid way. The church is not an autonomous being, he said, but the accumulation of the experiences of its members. As such it is living and moving. He found a way in his heart to do things like share communion with non-Catholics in such a manner as to be true both to his conscience and to his understanding of the underlying theology of the Eucharist.

This kind of religious talk was revolutionary to me. In my all-or-nothing approach I had never conceived of the church or its teachings as living, and thus things to be engaged with both heart and mind. Maybe it was time not for definitive answers but for waiting in the uncomfortable yet necessary place of uncertainty. This is what Henri encouraged me to do. Knowing that I was still in a place of doing more than being, Henri gave me a spiritual assignment that first week. I anticipated receiving Scripture passages to read or prayers to say, but Henri's advice was of a very different kind. "Spend some time in the chapel," he said. "But most of all, spend time with the core members, and just let them love you." Let them love me! This was the one thing I was not prepared for. But that advice proved to be truly life changing for me.

In each house I visited the core members welcomed me with open hearts. They had no expectations of me and didn't care about my seeming accomplishments. They were happy to share a smile or a joke, to sit and listen to music with me, or just to be in my company. I began to understand the essence of Henri's message. It isn't

Lisa Cataldo, Tracy Westerby, and Henri.

what we do or how much we can accomplish that makes us people of value. We are loved not because we are perfect but because we *are*—God is pleased by our being, and our being together.

I moved into the Daybreak community as a summer assistant a few months later and spent the next two summers at the Corner House with Tracy, Alia, Heather, and Hsi Fu. Each day, whether it brought laughter and joy or conflict and challenge, opened me to the gift of *being,* and Henri continued to be a big part of my journey. During those summers we went on meeting, and most of our talks centered on my evolving sense of my vocation. I had, with great encouragement from Henri, entered seminary the September after my first summer at Daybreak. Through my studies I gained a broader and more flexible understanding of church and vocation. But I still was not sure where God was calling me. Henri again and again called me back to the central questions. These were not about doctrine or denomination but about vocation—the call of God to each of us to grow into our true self, a person who reflects the image of God in a unique way.

In our meetings Henri and I talked of the many experiences that had brought me to this place in my life. I sometimes felt as if my diverse interests were just so much wandering around, avoiding a commitment. I continued to feel called to the priesthood, but the more I learned about myself and the church, the less sure I was that I could ever be anything but a Roman Catholic. As usual, Henri saw straight to the heart of the matter. He saw all my experiences as "stones in the road" of my spiritual journey. He felt sure that one day everything I had gained from my seeking would come together in a way that would allow me to live into my true vocation, whatever that turned out to be.

I continued to get caught up at times in the dilemma of doctrine. If I was a Catholic, what did that mean? One day Henri spoke to me at length, and beautifully, about the difference between doctrinal/political questions (he put these together) and deeper spiritual truth. He had come to believe that the sometimes conflicting questions that exist on one level all come together in God's unifying truth. While doctrines and opinions may look far apart on the surface, there is a deeper place of union, where it is clear that the apparent conflicts are not what really matter.

My own experience with meditation provided me with an understanding of Henri's belief, and I realized that I shared it. I knew I had, if only momentarily, walked in that place where all the questions are dissolved in the profound unity of God's love. But I felt far away from that then, and I was sure that for the time being I needed to engage the questions and all the uncertainty that came with them. Henri affirmed me in this and encouraged me always to engage my questions from the heart, with a view to that deeper place of unity.

Henri showed enormous patience with my struggle to discern the validity of my call to ordination and my concurrent attachment to the Catholic tradition. I wondered if I would ever *know* what I should do. It was around this issue that his advice was the most profound and unforgettable. While my mind was occupied with the question "to be ordained or not to be ordained?" Henri pointed out that perhaps my attachment to this question was itself a temptation to avoid a deeper issue. He said that by making this an either-or dilemma, I might be missing what God was trying to say about the *real* issue of my vocation. Ordination isn't really important, Henri claimed. I might be ordained or I might not; in the end it really wouldn't matter.

My sense of call was real, Henri said. Everything I told him about my deep longing to preach, to teach, and to celebrate the Eucharist confirmed that. Nothing any church officials said could keep me from being a priest in the community of believers—whether I wore a white collar or not. This brought me great comfort, but I still felt a need to *know* how things would turn out. Henri looked me in the eye, and in that look told me that he was truly seeing me, accepting me just as I was, anxiety and all. "Pursue the things you *do* know," he said, "and don't worry about what you don't know. What you don't know now may become clear to you, and it may not, but it is really not in your power to change that. Let God take care of the unknowns." He went on to say that the more we grow spiritually, the less far into the future we can see, yet the surer we are about doing the *next* right thing. "Such people have no idea what to do with their whole life," he said, "but they always seem to know what to do next."

Since I came to know Henri, my study of psychology has given me deeper insights into what our relationship was about. One of the most basic concepts of psychology is the "reality principle." Under the reality principle we grow to see people, events, objects, and organizations as they truly are and not as we wish them to be. We take back—often with considerable struggle—the myriad projections of our inner fears, wishes, and expectations that have colored our perceptions. We begin to see each individual as someone with fears, wishes, and expectations of his or her own and thus are able to enter into true relationship. The same idea can apply to our experience of an institution like the church. Through the reality principle we learn that neither people nor events and institutions are controlled by our fantasies. The encounter with the reality principle is not a one-time event but a process that continues throughout our lives. If we embrace it, our reward is a richer and more true engagement with life.

My relationship with Henri is one of the most important encounters with the reality principle that I have experienced. It
helped move me toward my chosen field of study and was certainly
a life lesson in the costs and rewards of seeing past the projection
to the real person. It was only by accepting the reality of Henri
that I was able to become more realistic about the church and my
vocation.

So who was the "real" Henri? This book contains many stories
by people who knew Henri variously as a pastor, a community
member, a writer, or a friend. Did we all know the same man? The
answer must be yes and no. Another idea in contemporary psychology helps illuminate this paradox. This concept proposes that
we are all multiple selves. While each of us has an image "me," that
thing we call self is multifaceted, presenting different dimensions
in each encounter. There is a way in which I am not the same Lisa
with my friends as with my parents or work colleagues or the
teenagers I teach. The more we grow into knowledge of ourselves,
the more we become aware that we are many selves, all of them
moving around the center point of our truest, deepest self, which
is perhaps known fully only by God.

In this way the Henri I knew was not the same Henri known
by Susan or Gord or Sally or Nathan. He was Henri-with-Lisa,
just as the facet of myself in our relationship was Lisa-with-Henri.
The coming together of these two individuals can never be dupli-
cated. In one way I would love to say I knew the "whole" Henri,
but I realize this is far from true. I accept our relationship as a
blessing in its uniqueness. For this is what we have with one another—moments of meeting between individuals who draw out
and in the best cases nurture and polish facets of the gem each of
us aspires to be. Each of my encounters with Henri was an encounter with life—deepening my understanding of my multifac-

eted self and the joyful and painful realities of relationship with a
multifaceted other.

When Carl called to tell me that Henri had died, I was heartbro-
ken along with thousands of others whose lives he touched. And
as on that day in the Dayspring kitchen, I was mad. I had grown
so much through my relationship with Henri. I had come to know
him as a person both strikingly flawed and profoundly gifted. He
had challenged my deepest-held projections and, by insisting on
being completely himself, allowed me to come to terms with both
his imperfections and my own. He had brought me into the Daybreak community, which I considered my family, and now he was
gone. Wasn't this just like Henri, to do something as inconsiderate
as desert me while I still needed his advice and guidance? I sat by
the phone and shouted at him. "Henri, what were you thinking?"

At Henri's funeral I sang in the choir and looked out at all the
people who had gathered to celebrate the intense, spectacular, and
too-short life of this complex and brilliant man. Many had known
Henri only through his books while others had seen him in his
multifaceted glory, where his woundedness and sometimes deep
sadness existed side by side with his overflowing energy and capacity for joy. I thought of the Henri I knew, the man who stood up
to my idealization and showed me some of the spectrum that made
up his true colors. Henri-with-Lisa was a being of great beauty,
one who with patience and love helped to nurture a more open,
and more realistic, person than I had been before.

The reality principle as I learned it through experience with
Henri certainly had its costs—my idealized image of the great
sage, as well as the very real loss of my friend—but its rewards
were incalculably more wonderful. These rewards were the fruits of

true relationship, with Henri and with myself. Because of the opportunity to be Lisa-with-Henri, I came to understand that the world of pat answers and perfect people is not the real world but only a fantasy whose attainment is not only impossible but undesirable. The true treasure is discovered, as Henri said, "when heart speaks to heart."

Today I am pursuing a doctorate in psychology and religion, with an emphasis on the psychological and spiritual function of play in our worship of God. I teach religion part-time in a Catholic high school and have become comfortable with myself as a Roman Catholic, though I remain deeply ecumenical in my spirituality. The ordination question has transformed itself into a commitment to educate and pray for growth in understanding among church leaders so that women will one day be welcome to full participation in the sacraments. I consider my "renunciation" of my call to ordination a sacrifice necessary to retain my voice in the Roman Catholic Church and a commitment to solidarity with all Catholic women. At the same time I remain open to God's call, knowing that it may lead me in new and surprising directions.

My relationship with Henri did not end with his death. I often seek his advice when my path seems confusing or a particular challenge feels like too much. Invariably, I can hear his gurgling, Dutch-colored English as he says to me, "Don't worry about what to do with the rest of your life. Just be yourself, and let God love you." And every time, it is enough.

He's a Good
Teacher to Me

GORDON HENRY

*Gordon Henry came to L'Arche Daybreak in 1972. For the past fifteen years
he has worked at the Woodery. Henri was Gord's spiritual director. He invited Gord to accompany him sometimes when he taught or spoke at special
events. Gord asked John Guido to interview him for this contribution.*

John: Tell me about the course you taught with Henri.

*Gord, Henri, and Carl MacMillan
at a formal dinner.*

Gord: We talked about the
Prodigal Son, about how the father holds the son. I talked to the
people, "Try to open your heart."

J: What was your relationship
with Henri?

G: He's a good teacher to me.
I went to see him before work.
Pretty often. Henri said, "Just
open your heart." Help me get my
feelings out.

The way I see it, Henri cared

Henri and Gord Henry in conversation.

about me, about temptations. Henri said, "You see a wallet there. What are you going to do? Tell someone about it. Don't steal." He told me, "Be yourself, Gordie. You care about people." I feel a bit strong. So nice that Henri took me out for a beer. "Don't get drunk, Gordie." After talking to Henri I found it a bit peaceful. Henri visited me in hospital. He's taking me on a train in Holland. He takes me to see his friends. I really come close to Henri's family.

Henri says nice words. Help me get my anger out, talk to God. Henri was a good friend to me. He cared about my family.

J: What kind of a man was Henri?

G: He was always peaceful. He was a little bit deaf—not too much. "Speak up, Gordie. Be yourself." I remember Henri's birthday was in January. Henri was a clown. Lots of guests. He was happy.

I find it a little bit hard now. I wish Henri would be here to tell stories about me. Henri, you know, he's a sweetheart; he's great.

ON HOSPITALITY

Hospitality means primarily the creation of a free space where the stranger can enter and become a friend instead of an enemy. Hospitality is not to change people, but to offer them space where change can take place. It is not to bring men and women over to our side, but to offer freedom not disturbed by dividing lines. It is not to lead our neighbor into a corner where there are no alternatives left, but to open a wide spectrum of options for choice and commitment. It is not an educated intimidation with good books, good stories and good works, but the liberation of fearful hearts so that words can find roots and bear ample fruit. It is not a method of making our God and our way into the criteria of happiness, but the opening of an opportunity to others to find their God and their way. The paradox of hospitality is that it wants to create emptiness, not a fearful emptiness, but a friendly emptiness where strangers can enter and discover themselves as created free; free to sing their own songs, speak their own languages, dance their own dances; free also to leave and follow their own vocations. Hospitality is not a subtle invitation to adopt the life style of the host, but the gift of a chance for the guest to find his own.

—Reaching Out

Henri, Mamie, and Us

JOHN FRASER

John Fraser and his wife, Elizabeth MacCallum, met Henri through Mme. Pauline Vanier, Jean Vanier's mother, at the original L'Arche community in France, where she spent her retirement. Mamie, as she was affectionately known in L'Arche, was former first lady of Canada. (Her husband, Georges, had been governor-general.) When Henri came to Daybreak, John and Elizabeth were back in Toronto. John, a well-known Canadian writer and editor, is master of Massey College at the University of Toronto.

The first sight Elizabeth and I ever had of Henri was in August 1985 in Mamie Vanier's living room at the L'Arche community in Trosly-Breuil, France. He was staying in her gracious home for the year, and she had welcomed him immediately into her heart even as she had us some years earlier. Henri had just left his teaching post at Harvard University and was searching for direction in his life. L'Arche was almost the exact opposite of the university culture he had left behind, and, in learning to relate to people who could neither read nor speak, he was on shaky ground. But he and Mamie were kindred spirits: well read, intelligent, and strong extroverts. Often they would sit together over a meal conversing about his experiences in L'Arche, about world events, and about their own human struggles. She loved the Eucharist and was overjoyed to have it celebrated by Henri in her home. Daily they would each invite a few people to these intimate times of communion.

Mamie's home was an anchor for Henri that year and during his subsequent visits to Trosly. He told us once that he always felt happier after he left Mamie. I think she was a kind of touchstone for him. For her part, Mamie was dealing with the hardships of aging and a certain loneliness in the midst of a busy community. So it was a mutually nourishing relationship. She always said she got so much from Henri, but in truth her combination of tea and sympathy provided a large part of his sense of well-being.

Before our first meeting Mamie had set Henri up as "a deeply spiritual man," and she did it in such a way that I was immediately curious and perhaps a bit jealous. Talk about falling into a Nouwen trap! When I told Henri much later that I had harbored dark feelings about the influence he seemed to have over Mamie's spiritual landscape, he gave me a big hug and laughed so much he made us laugh. In fact, my confession of this selfish little trait made us closer friends.

On that first occasion, Henri listened as Elizabeth and I gossiped with Mamie about international affairs and about China, where I had been working, and then a chance comment shifted the moment out of geopolitics into tales of our children. A story we told him about our eldest daughter, Jessie, and a prayer she had composed threatening God with dire retribution filled him with curiosity and wonder.

Suddenly he became a reporter. What was the incident? he asked. At our family cottage, Jessie, age five, had found a dead sparrow and arranged a coffin, shroud, procession with cross, and an entire funeral service. "Dear God," she'd intoned at the grave site, "we have buried this little sparrow. Now you be good to it or I'll kill you. Amen." Elizabeth had said, "Jessie, you don't have to threaten God," and Jessie replied that she just wanted "to make sure" God looked after the bird.

Henri transformed this into a spiritual insight of charming directness. It's in *The Road to Daybreak,* which we keep close to us in our library, along with a picture of Jessie as a little girl tucked in at the page of the anecdote. Today Jessie is a vibrant young woman, but she is also still alive to us as the little girl in this story, in the same way Henri is still alive as the compassionate companion he was for so many people.

We saw Henri on many occasions after that first encounter. It was always a joy to travel to Daybreak in Richmond Hill. To be at mass with him there was perfect bliss. We had so wanted to share him with the people we'd worshiped among since our marriage. It was not to be, but thoughts of him come to us often in our parish church, and, in ways that seem very real, he makes the trip to our sanctuary repeatedly—and always with open arms and that smile that lit up the universe.

Mamie's funeral at the cathedral in Quebec City in 1991 was not our last encounter with Henri before he died, but to my mind it was the most significant later encounter. This was because we were burying the woman who had meant so much to all of us, and the pain of the departure was keen. Mamie's son Jean spoke, and as it was a state funeral, the current governor-general of Canada came. As we lived through that day we talked with Henri about our shared memories of Mamie, and he agreed with us that her little living room and dining room at Trosly was a very special sanctuary, her cigarettes providing the incense and her gingerbread cake and tea the very matrix of a domestic communion.

We gathered around the cold stone face of the rock where Mamie's mortal remains were about to join those of her beloved Georges, at the heart of the Citadel. As we held hands all around her, Henri started us singing the Taizé chant "Ubi Caritas"— where there is love, God is present—and we could feel her soul's warm graciousness envelop us. But gradually I also realized it was Henri who was willing her presence among us, and that was so appropriate because he had come to her rescue—the phrase was Mamie's own—sharing her house and sharing the Eucharist when she needed him. Now he had given us the means to say good-bye, and this was only one of the incalculable gifts that had come our way from this good and decent and God-filled man.

How we miss him! How grateful we are for our memories of him.

ON CELEBRATION

Celebration lifts up not only the happy moments but the sad moments as well. . . . Celebration is not a party on special occasions, but an ongoing awareness that every moment is special and asks to be lifted up and recognized as a blessing from on high. . . .

Celebration is not just a way to make people feel good for a while; it is the way in which faith in the God of life is lived out, through both laughter and tears. Thus celebration goes beyond ritual, custom, and tradition. It is the unceasing affirmation that underneath all the ups and downs of life there flows a solid current of joy. The handicapped men and women of L'Arche are becoming my teachers in the most important course of all: living in the house of God. Their joy leads me beyond the fearful place of death, and opens my eyes to the ecstatic potential of all life. Joy offers the solid ground from which new life can always burst. Joy can be caught neither in one feeling or emotion nor in one ritual or custom but is always more than we expect, always surprising, and therefore always a sign that we are in the presence of the Lord of life.

—*Lifesigns*

A Man of Creative Contradictions

PETER NAUS

Peter Naus and Henri became friends during their student days in Holland. Peter came to the United States to teach psychology at the University of Notre Dame in South Bend, Indiana, while Henri was there. He later taught at St. Jerome's University in Waterloo, Ontario. Now a professor emeritus, he lives with his wife, Anke, in Kitchener, Ontario.

I knew Henri for almost forty years. We met in 1957, when we were both students in psychology at the Catholic University of Nijmegen in the Netherlands. Henri had close ties to my family for a long time. He married us and baptized our oldest son. He married our youngest son, and he assisted at the wedding of our oldest son. Were it not for Henri we might never have moved to North America. While Henri was teaching at the newly established department of psychology at the University of Notre Dame, he proposed to the chair that I be invited as a visiting professor for a year. After I obtained my doctorate, I returned to America and to Notre Dame.

Henri and I did not have much in common initially. He was

several years older and a priest. He came from a well-educated and rather well-to-do family while mine was blue-collar; I was the first in my family to attend university. He was urbanized and cultured. I, by contrast, grew up in a small village and was struggling to adjust to a social milieu that was rather foreign to me. I had been fortunate enough to meet a mentor in high school who introduced me to classical music and other forms of art. Henri continued this process. He also invited me on several occasions to have dinner with his parents. We never talked about this explicitly, but I think Henri sensed my difficulties with the clash between my own social background and the university environment, and he took initiatives that eased the transition for me. One of the many debts I owe him is for this help.

Henri was also instrumental in the maturing of my faith. He agreed to give instruction to my fiancée, Anke, who wanted to become a Roman Catholic. The three of us met for almost a year in 1958, and our sessions had a lasting impact on me. Henri paid little attention to church dogma or to rules and conventions. Instead, he made the teachings of Christ his focus. I was forced to reexamine my own faith, which was the product of a highly conservative religious upbringing. I challenged Henri many times when I thought there was a contradiction between what I had been taught to believe and what he propagated. Gently and patiently he loosened my rigid and unyielding faith stance and helped me shift from a preoccupation with external practices based on dogmatic beliefs to the exploration of a personal connection with Christ. While our sessions were meant to guide Anke's conversion, in many ways they brought about my own conversion as well.

I am rather certain that Henri's instruction was different from those current at the time. He was more daring, less conventional, more pastoral than other priests I knew. That has always surprised me, especially when I discovered his almost scrupulous fear of deviating from church teaching and altering church rituals, though this fear abated in later years.

Despite our frequent contacts, I did not get to know Henri intimately. Apart from discussing our religious beliefs, our conversations were seldom personal. We talked about our studies and his many extracurricular activities. My impression of Henri as intense and always on the go was formed early in our relationship. He was usually center stage in the projects in which he was involved. This was often not appreciated by his fellow students or by some of his teachers. Although generalizations are dangerous and national character is a nebulous concept, it is fair to say that the Dutch see virtue in not standing out. Those who do stand out often face ridicule, though it is not always expressed directly. In fact, I do not remember that Henri was criticized openly; he simply did not receive proper recognition.

What many found particularly irritating was Henri's tendency to rub shoulders with the powerful; some saw him as a social climber. I found myself often defending him because I did not agree with what I considered a misrepresentation of his motives fueled by plain envy. Henri was intrigued by anything out of the ordinary, and he was extremely curious about people, including those in positions of power and prestige. I do not believe he wanted to raise his own status by associating with these individuals. I did not, however, realize at the time how much the misunderstanding and criticism he encountered might have hurt him because I only discovered much later how vitally important it was for him to be accepted and respected.

The reactions and feelings Henri faced as a student foreshadowed the reception his lecturing and writing would receive in his home country a number of years hence, even though the reasons for the lukewarm response were more complicated then. They had to do with changes in Dutch Roman Catholicism and were based on perceptions of Henri's position regarding these changes. His unwillingness to criticize publicly the church hierarchy did not sit well with some, and his spirituality was seen as overly simplistic and pious.

His lecturing style was also rather foreign to Dutch audiences. His penchant for expressive, often theatrical, gestures and the high energy level of his talks made Dutch people, especially those who considered themselves educated, feel uncomfortable. Certainly in academic circles, emotional restraint, precise, logical development, and careful presentation of ideas were considered hallmarks of a good lecture; there was little room for spontaneity and exuberance. In recent years things have changed in Holland. Younger generations appear more open, less self-conscious, more nonconformist. Despite the ongoing secularization of Dutch society (or because of it), interest in spirituality—as distinct from religiosity—has increased. These are some of the reasons for the growing appreciation and recognition of Henri's work in his native country, although he never came close there to the popularity he enjoyed in North America, especially the United States.

My relationship with Henri became more personal, more truly a friendship, while we were colleagues at Notre Dame. I saw Henri no longer as my spiritual guide but as someone with whom I could have fun and share ideas. As it turned out, sharing ideas was a lot easier than having fun. It was indeed rather difficult to get Henri to relax and enjoy whatever was coming his way.

Over the next fifteen to twenty years we had regular contact by phone or face-to-face. Henri shared with me his joys and satisfactions, but also his suffering and disappointments. Although he did not always seek my advice, he included me whenever he had to make important decisions, such as leaving Yale University and, probably his most important decision, leaving academia altogether to join the L'Arche community of Daybreak.

Besides his effect on my career and my faith, Henri's vision of education and teaching influenced me, if only because it supported my own evolving notions. He insisted that teaching should be noncompetitive and reciprocal. He taught me to rely more on my own insights and experience when giving a lecture and to leave a prepared text to become more responsive to the reactions of an audience. His understandings and descriptions of friendship, parenthood, loneliness, forgiveness, and many other aspects of the human condition proved invaluable in my teaching and research. Since the first time he mentioned it I have been intrigued by the idea that intimate relationships should be hospitable and inclusive. That is probably why I was so moved when he described the relationship between our youngest son and his bride as hospitable in his homily at their wedding. His concept of the wounded healer was central to my view of caring and became a focal point of the course I taught on aging, dying, and death. Henri never ceased to encourage me to write. His feedback was supportive and precise.

I have always felt much affinity for Henri's dialectical thinking, examples of which abound in his writing. Consider this quotation from *Out of Solitude*, one of his earliest books:

> *It seems that there is no clear-cut joy, but that even in the most happy moments of our existence we sense a tinge of sadness. In every satisfaction, there is an awareness of its limitations. In every success there is the fear of jealousy. Behind every smile, there is a tear. In every em-*

brace, there is loneliness. In every friendship, distance. And in all forms of light, there is the knowledge of surrounding darkness.

Often the dialectical opposition he identified was between something undesirable and something desirable, for instance, between teaching as a violent process and teaching as a redemptive process, between a life in action and a life in solitude, or between competition and compassion.

According to Henri, teaching becomes a violent process when it takes place in a context where competition is prized, the interaction between teacher and students is primarily unidirectional, and students become alienated from themselves and others because school is seen as preparation for later life rather than as a setting for exploring their experiences here and now. In contrast, teaching is redemptive when it is evocative, bilateral, and actualizing. That is, when it is aimed at drawing upon the experiences and talents of teacher and students; when it recognizes that teachers can learn from students; and that learning for the future is based in understanding and appreciating interactions here and now.

Henri's own life exemplified the dialectical opposition between living in action and living in solitude. Living in action means being preoccupied with achievement and success, whether in work or in one's social interactions, or even in one's spiritual life. By contrast, living in solitude means—to use his words—to "discover in the center of your own self that we are not what we can conquer, but what is given to us." It means acknowledging that who we are transcends our achievements.

Henri spoke and wrote often about the pervasiveness of competition in our world. Feeling insecure, anxious, and vulnerable, people understandably want to distinguish themselves from others in order to attain some measure of self-regard. Yet Henri called upon us to resist the temptation to establish our differentness and urged us instead to value our common humanity. To be compassionate—to suffer with—should be more desirable to us than to make a difference or excel.

Henri did not suggest that the movement from one dialectical pole to the other was all-or-nothing or to be achieved once and for all. He believed that we are capable of transformation but not without struggle and not without a constant temptation to return to our old ways. Henri knew this from his own experience. For instance, from the outset he wrote and spoke eloquently of the dangers of seeking success and approval, yet he could never quite manage to stop worrying about the reception of his books and he remained overly sensitive to the approval of others. There is a very revealing passage in *Out of Solitude:*

> *Once in a while someone will confess in an intimate moment, "Everyone thinks I am very quiet and composed, but if only they knew how I really feel. . . ." This nagging self-doubt is at the basis of so much depression in the lives of many people who are struggling in our competitive society. Moreover, this corroding fear for the discovery of our weaknesses prevents community and creative sharing. When we have sold our identity to the judges of this world, we are bound to become restless, because of a growing need for affirmation and praise. Indeed we are tempted to become low-hearted because of our constant self-rejection. And we are in serious danger of becoming isolated, since friendship and love are impossible without a mutual vulnerability.*

How true! But is it not rather obvious that Henri himself was the "someone" making the confession?

Henri's life was full of tensions, contradictions, and inconsistencies. The most tragic yet most creative contradiction was implied in his inability to live out what he wrote. This was a source of great sadness for him and a reason for some to question the validity of his ideas and his credibility as a spiritual guide. The paradox is that he would never have become an inspirational spiritual writer if he had lived what he wrote. Therefore, his personal tragedy was also his gift to others.

Why was it so difficult for Henri to live by his own spiritual directives? I am not sure, but clearly his intense need for affirmation was a key factor. Why was this need never satisfied, despite the overwhelming approval, affection, and love bestowed upon him? For some the answer is obvious: Henri was gay, and since he did not allow himself to enter into an emotional/sexual relationship with another man, his affective and sexual needs remained frustrated. I have always believed that his reasons for being gay and the underlying dynamics were extremely complicated and far from transparent. As I see it, the primary issue in Henri's case was not his sexual orientation but a deep-seated insecurity, a sense that he was not securely connected to the people around him, including the significant others in his life. I have often wondered about the source of this insecurity but never found a convincing answer. The only thing I am certain of is that it lay in the distant past.

Henri struggled with this insecurity all his life. It caused him sometimes to make unreasonable demands on his friends and to place expectations on a specific friendship that were impossible to meet. Just when it appeared that he had finally discovered at Daybreak the home he had been looking for ever since he left his family home as a teenager, he was overwhelmed by feelings of utter desolation and abandonment. He thought he had found in a friendship with one of the members of that community the connection he had so long sought. When this friendship appeared to have broken, Henri was shattered. Intellectually, he knew that neither this friendship nor any other could satisfy his yearning for connection, but emotionally he was unable to accept it. Henri came to visit me at this darkest moment of his life. Whatever insight our conversation gave him into his situation, it did nothing to relieve his anguish and despair. I could only hope and pray that the therapy he was seeking would be effective. As it turned out, he overcame his depression and the friendship was restored. Although his insecurity and the vulnerabilities connected to it had not disappeared, the powerful combination of psychological therapy and spiritual healing he received helped him to recognize more clearly these vulnerabilities and, more important, taught him to live with them constructively and creatively.

Henri's restlessness, inner tensions, and neediness are part of the image and memory I have of our friendship, but they do not dominate. There may not have been enough lightness in Henri's life, not because he was tormented and unhappy all the time but because he was overly earnest and serious. Precisely because there were not enough of them, I remember with fondness occasions when he was relaxed and playful. One of my earliest recollections is of the party he gave when he graduated from university. It was fun to see him so clearly enjoying the moment. The party ended with a dance to "La Bamba"; Henri gave a rousing rendition! I remember also the party at Daybreak to celebrate his sixtieth birthday. He seemed to relish all the attention and affection. It was one of those times when Henri's endearing childlike qualities came to the fore.

This also happened when he was playing with children or when he received presents he liked. For several years my wife and I used to give him a sweater on his birthday, either one knitted by Anke or one we bought. He would try it on immediately and prance around in it. Although he often looked a little disheveled, he enjoyed wearing attractive clothes, not so much because they might improve his appearance but because they were sensually and aesthetically pleasing. That is one thing Henri and I had in common! It is one of the many paradoxes of Henri's personality that his earnestness was paired with childlike qualities.

Henri was an excellent storyteller, especially because he had a great sense of drama and perfect timing. It was delightful to hear about his trips and the many interesting people he met. He often spiced up these stories by recounting humorous events. He loved to laugh. I remember he and Anke and I listening to tapes of Dutch comedians. He was drawn to clowns, the genuine ones whose ability to laugh and get others to laugh stems from their sensitivity to the tragic side of human existence and an astute sense of their own brokenness. There was a "clownish" side to Henri that fit his own description of clowns in *Clowning in Rome*:

> *The clowns don't have it together, they do not succeed in what they try, they are awkward, out of balance and left-handed, but . . . they are on our side. We respond to them not with admiration but with sympathy, not with amazement but with understanding, not with tension but with a smile. Of the virtuosi we say, "How can they do it?" Of the clowns we say, "They are like us."*

Henri was a generous man. He always made himself available to others and he shared his material possessions freely. He never expected anything in return except a simple recognition for the favor or gift.

I think of Henri often. Sometimes I feel guilty for not having been more faithful to our friendship. But mostly I feel grateful for having known Henri. I feel grateful for his guidance and inspiration; I feel grateful for what he taught me, by instruction and example, about the human condition, about its many contradictions, its moments of pure joy and deepest despair, its extreme vulnerability and strong resiliency; I feel grateful for his showing me by example that faith in God is possible, even if God's presence is often not tangible; most of all I am grateful for a relationship that helped me build my strengths and accept my weaknesses.

ON PERSONAL
CHANGE AND
COMMUNITY

Your own growth cannot take place without growth in others. You are part of a body. When you change, the whole body changes. It is very important for you to remain deeply connected with the larger community to which you belong.

It is also important that those who belong to the body of which you are a part keep faith in your journey. You still have a way to go, and there will be times when your friends are puzzled or even disillusioned by what is happening to you. At certain moments things may seem more difficult for you than before; they may look worse than when you began. You still have to make the great passage, and that might not happen without a lot of new distress and fear. Through all of this, it is important for you to stay united with the larger body and know that your journey is made not just for yourself but for all who belong to the body.

Think about Jesus. He made his journey and asked his disciples to follow him even where they would rather not go. The journey you are choosing is Jesus' journey, and whether or not you are fully aware of it, you are also asking your brothers and sisters to follow you. Somewhere you already know that what you are living now will not leave the other members of the community untouched. Your choices also call your friends to make new choices.

— *The Inner Voice of Love*

A Covenant of
Friendship

NATHAN BALL

*Nathan Ball met Henri at L'Arche in Trosly-Breuil, France, in 1985, and
they soon developed a close friendship. They both came to L'Arche Daybreak the
following year. There, Nathan completed a master of divinity degree and in
1990 became community leader. He and his wife, Paula Kilcoyne, live with
their daughter, Emmanuelle, and her younger sister, Anna-Claire, in Richmond Hill, Ontario.*

I'm writing from the Benedictine monastery in Erie, Pennsylvania,
where my wife Paula, our baby, Emmanuelle, and I have come for
a week of retreat. Having made a number of retreats as a single
person, I am eager to enter into this week with my family. I anticipate a period of personal and family renewal and, through our
time together, new insight into the spirituality of marriage and
family.

I live these days of retreat close to Henri. In many ways he has
shaped the vision and practice of my spiritual life. His passion for
living a spiritual life, his unceasing desire to be faithful, the courageous and creative way he encountered his own suffering and responded to the suffering of others, and his vision and capacity for

spiritual friendship—all have made lasting marks upon me. As a young man searching and struggling to make basic life choices but confused by the many divergent voices in and around me, I found in Henri a friend, a priest, a mentor, a colleague, and, in each of these roles, someone who loved me more deeply than I could receive.

Henri's love was far from perfect. Both he and others have written about the particular constellation of psychospiritual energies that made Henri a challenging person to relate to at times. But the transformation that happened for me within the context of our friendship happened not in spite of Henri's weaknesses and struggles but precisely because he engaged me in a direct and unabashed manner with the whole of who he was. Neither my current vision for life nor my capacity to stay in the struggle to live a fruitful life would be what it is today apart from Henri.

I also live these days of retreat close to Henri because I am still integrating the impact that his life, his friendship, and his death have had on me. Some friendships, and ours was one, pass through a purifying suffering before they manifest a more mutual and selfless commitment to the personal and spiritual development of the other. There was a time when the mixture of our personal limitations precipitated a crisis of friendship, which I at first thought would be terminal. But through a slow and sometimes excruciatingly painful process that is as yet incomplete for me, significant personal change occurred for both of us. In various ways Henri has spoken of our friendship. In this essay I want to witness to how Henri has shaped my life. My purpose is not to romanticize or idealize our relationship but to focus intentionally on the great gift that Henri's life is for me.

. . .

We met in the fall of 1985. He, Dutch, Roman Catholic, and fifty-five years of age. I, Canadian, Protestant by heritage, twenty-eight, and as highly introverted as he was extroverted. We were both away from home, living in the original community of L'Arche in France. In the preceding years some signal events had happened in my life: I had helped found a small ecumenical community; I had come to know the L'Arche community in Calgary; my brother Tim had died; and I had joined the Roman Catholic Church. I was deeply touched by some of the people with developmental disabilities in L'Arche and by my brother's life and too early death due to a brain tumor. I had been working as the manager of a bookstore, but I knew this was not my vocation. This time at L'Arche in France was an opportunity to explore what all of this meant for me and seek direction.

Henri and I each knew that our stays in France would be temporary, but neither of us yet sensed what would come next. We knew only that we had come to L'Arche in response to an inner call and that each of us was discerning the next phase of his life. Neither of us ever imagined that for the next twelve years our inner and outer lives would become inexplicably interwoven as we discovered, individually and together, a call to friendship and a call to become part of the mission of L'Arche that would be lived out in the community of L'Arche Daybreak.

As a heterosexual man I was a safe person for Henri to love deeply, and I in turn was eager for his friendship and companionship. In retrospect it is clear to me that we needed each other. We were able to support each other in concrete ways: Henri in his desire to be faithful to his vow of celibacy as a Roman Catholic priest and I in the hope that I would grow in my capacity for intimacy and commitment and might one day marry.

We experienced an immediate connection of mind and heart,

though the latter meeting place was where we spent most of our time: two restless and often anxious hearts that recognized each other as potential friends and soul mates. I remember the resonance with which we read together a passage from the twelfth-century monk William of St. Thierry that describes a dynamic at the center of the human experience: "Nothing can be so restless and fleeting—no part of my nature can be so changeful—than my heart. How exceedingly vain, trifling, wandering, and unsettled is this vagabond."

We were both men with open hearts who had made a clear choice to follow Jesus in his way of love and service. And we each knew that dealing directly with the reality of our restless hearts was an integral part of this spiritual journey. Still, it was with surprise that we began talking, very early on, about our mutual experience that this unlikely friendship was being given so that each of us would grow in faithfulness to life in the Spirit and in our ability to live well in the world of relationships and work.

I was drawn to Henri quickly and, at the beginning, without reservation. He was so alive, an enfleshed spirit who moved in and out and around people and ideas with amazing speed and dexterity. I knew little about him. I met him at an English-language Eucharist. Shortly after, he visited the L'Arche home where I lived, and soon we were getting to know each other. I can still, all these years later, reach out and touch the moment when, over a long dinner in a small bistro in the nearby city of Compiègne, our friendship began. I can see the childlike twinkle in his eye as he tells a funny story, the intense interest with which he is listening to me, and our mutual appreciation of the red wine. I see his large hands wrapped around the wineglass like a blanket, hands that I would eventually come to know as the barometer of his soul—hands that would give a warm embrace or a reassuring pat on the back, hands clasping a chalice and lifted up in praise and thanksgiving, or fingers that would sometimes bleed from being scratched and picked, visible expressions of an inner anguish. The trustworthy and intensely personal way he communicated made long conversation easy for me.

It was with Henri that I discovered how nurturing it could be to go on retreat with another person. I recall the first retreat we made together. I had four days free, and Henri proposed we go to Rheims. We stayed in a monastery close to the cathedral, which has a striking stained-glass window by Marc Chagall. Henri had a gentle vision of how to live such retreats. The saying of morning and evening prayer framed the day. Times of silence and solitary prayer were supported by times of faith-sharing between friends. Our retreats had a confessional quality as we explored what it means to foster a supportive spiritual friendship. A quiet walk together would often punctuate the late afternoon. I was always enthusiastic, as was Henri, about these periods away. His desire for time apart and his thirst for an active life of prayer including daily Eucharist drew me into a place of spiritual intimacy that I could not easily access on my own.

As our friendship progressed we discovered a number of common interests, not the least of which was the project of living in community, building community life, and exercising leadership in a Christian community. Another reason we were drawn to each other was our mutual need for friendship that actively supported living a spiritual life. Henri's insistence that it is not possible to live the spiritual life alone helped call me out from my own place of passivity in relationship to both people and God. As is often the case with friends, we found a bond in this common endeavor of developing a spiritual friendship.

Both of us were concerned about issues of meaning. We would

talk about how to sustain a supportive friendship that would enable us to live relevant spiritual lives in our times. I knew that if I stayed in L'Arche I would likely be called to leadership of some kind. What are the elements that enable a person to remain emotionally and affectively well in a life of service? I was not at all sure I would marry, but neither did I know how I could live well as a single person. I experienced our friendship as an anchor, a place where loving encouragement was given, challenges offered, and insights shared. And I began to feel more courageous in response to my own trials and temptations.

Our friendship was rooted as much in our differences as in our similarities. I was fascinated by the enormous energy Henri had for life. He was interested in everyone and everything. And the fact that he was much more emotional than I only served as a welcome beacon that drew me into a more intentional engagement with my own inner world. Within this evolving friendship I began to give new expression to some of my deeply held hopes and dreams. Experiences of sadness, disappointment, and shame were brought into a sacred place of love. These were healing moments, for which I will always be grateful. Henri's responsiveness to me, heart-filled and soulful, a responsiveness I saw offered also to so many others, became a new inspiration for my relationships with others.

When I reflect on how my inner life and spiritual desire have been affected by Henri, two words come to the fore: fidelity and suffering. So often and in so many ways, Henri expressed his desire to be faithful—faithful to God, to his own inner self, to the demands of love, to friendships, and to his chosen vocation as a priest. He encouraged and challenged me to hold this vision of faithfulness with him and to allow it to be the vision that permeated all I do.

Certainly it was obvious that I, as he, would not always be faithful, that trust would fail, and that breakages would occur. But the desire to be faithful was always the critical starting place for Henri.

This was never clearer than during the period of time, a little over a year after we had come to Daybreak, when our friendship broke down. Unable to bear the expectations we had put upon each other, we entered into a long period of silence before a slow rebuilding of the trust and friendship that had earlier been so obvious and available to us. It was an agonizing time which provoked serious questions within me. How could something so right go so wrong? As was evidenced in our other relationships, we both had a capacity to sustain friendship. And had not our friendship been given to us so that we could be faithful to the call of God in our lives? Where was God now?

I took consolation in other friendships and sought counseling to better understand my part in this painful break. But I was deeply moved by a letter from Henri in which he reaffirmed his trust in and dependence upon God even when he understood, as did I, that we might never recover our friendship. His desire to be faithful to the spirit of God in the midst of our crisis was paramount: "Under the many waves of anguish and torment, I experience a deep gratitude to God . . . and I want to let you know that I believe with all my heart that Jesus has indeed given us to each other and that what Jesus has done is of lasting significance for both of us."

Henri returned after some months away from Daybreak, and slowly, with the support of others and with struggle, trust between us began to regrow; a new, clearer, and more realistic formulation of our expectations of each other became possible, and we were able to resume our friendship. It was shaky at times, and I recall, after I became community leader, realizing that if our friendship failed again the break would be definitive and come at considerable cost to the community. But we stayed in the struggle, and our doing so may have been a model for others. By the early 1990s our friendship was on a much more solid footing.

Henri's role as pastor of Daybreak was important to me. For six years we worked together as colleagues. We shared a common conviction about the importance of L'Arche in our society, and we sought to ensure a unified vision between the administrative and spiritual aspects of the community. We were able to support and challenge each other to provide the kind of leadership the community needed, and when the inevitable crises of community life arose we could confer helpfully. It was a very fruitful period in Daybreak's development, a time when the community grew in both size and depth and became more spiritually rooted.

We continued our custom of making periodic short retreats together. I knew I could have a better retreat if I did not just go alone, and Henri, whose need for these times was more intense than mine, had a good sense of how to live them fruitfully. Sometimes we would simply slip off for a day or two to a nearby retreat center. We would each bring work but would take time to pray together, talk, and celebrate the Eucharist.

The question of particular friendships has always been problematic within community, and this continues to be the case in L'Arche. But we had a strong desire to be faithful to the double call of friendship and the responsible exercise of leadership within our community. With the support of others we grew in our ability to hold these two calls together in a creative tension.

I went through periods when Henri's importance to me as priest-confessor and spiritual guide was more pronounced. When I joined the Roman Catholic Church, I had not been confirmed. Henri prepared me for confirmation, and we celebrated this at Pentecost in 1994. At another time he directed me on a private eight-

Nathan Ball (center) with Joe Vorstermans and Henri on the beach at Cancún.

day retreat, driving daily to a nearby retreat center to meet with me. And I was often inspired by homilies he gave during community worship.

We also made some wonderful trips together—to Calgary to visit my family, to Cancún in Mexico with Joe Vorstermans for a philanthropy conference. There I wanted to treat Henri to a parasail ride, but he insisted we do the ride together—a memorable and hilarious experience. Henri could be so adventuresome and often joyful and enthusiastic about life. A couple of years before his death we met for a relaxing tour of Holland, where Henri introduced me to his family and friends and some of the important places of his early adulthood. One of the poignant moments was a visit we made to his mother's grave.

I will always think of Henri as a suffering servant. His huge heart, held within his vocation of priest, was constantly open to the suffering of others. His own personal suffering, often triggered by feelings of rejection, isolation, or abandonment, was equally large. I came to see his capacity to suffer as an expression of his unusual human capacity, and this in turn called me to a greater maturity both in relationship to my own struggles and in my emerging sense of vocation. Henri longed to be faithful to God's covenant with him through the nurture of covenant relationships—relationships of deep commitment. The ability to stay in the reality of suffering was for him the heart of the matter. Even after having lived close to Henri for a number of years, I still find this model for living deeply challenging. But I do know that I am a gentler, kinder person who has been given a powerful living example of how to stay in touch with the reality of human existence.

The constancy of Henri's commitment to me as a person, the risks he took in the service of our friendship, and the enormous effort he made to support new growth for both of us called those same qualities out of me. But for me it went further. This relationship and its inspiration for me was a critical factor in the slow but steady growth in my ability to trust myself, my desires, and, most of all, my capacity to love. Henri's fidelity to me has helped me choose the way of fidelity for my life. The directness with which he related to the suffering in and around him has helped me to be more open and less afraid of my own struggles and those of the people around me.

From the beginning I experienced Henri as a connector, someone who brought people together, who pointed the way toward connection with God, and who loved to develop insights connecting God's love with human experience. I will always be grateful for the spaces of my heart that have been opened because of Henri. In expressing this gratitude, I know that I am pointing to how the mystery of God visited me through Henri's life, death, and witness.

My Christmases
with Henri

PATSY RAMSAY

Patsy Ramsay has been a core member at L'Arche Daybreak since 1974. She enjoys participating in a theater group and a day program. Henri remains a strong figure in Patsy's memory, and she reminds others of special times with him. Patsy asked Cheryl Zinyk to help her prepare this contribution.

Patsy spent three Christmases with Henri, Sue Mosteller, and Elizabeth Buckley. On Christmas Day at breakfast, Patsy would sit op-

*Patsy (center) with Sue, Elizabeth,
and Henri.*

posite Henri and tell him he was "beautiful and handsome," and Henri would laugh with delight and say, "Nobody ever called me that before!" Patsy reflected on this Christmas picture taken at the Dayspring in 1990.

Patsy: Oh! There is Henri, myself, Sue, and Elizabeth.

Cheryl: What did you do?

P: Christmas . . . have meals . . . sit around, open presents.

C: What did you like about spending time with Henri?

P: Oh, he's so handsome.

C: Did Henri like you?

P: Yes! He liked me a lot. He's cute and sweet. I liked him. He's nice.

Then Patsy drew this picture of herself and Henri by the Christmas tree.

Connie and Henri: A Spiritual Compatibility

STEVE AND CARMEN ELLIS

Steve and Carmen Ellis are the son and daughter-in-law of Connie Ellis, Henri's first secretary at L'Arche Daybreak and a good friend until she died in 1994. Steve and Carmen have been involved in L'Arche for many years. This contribution is based on a tape-recorded conversation with Philip Coulter. Carmen, like Steve, refers to Connie as "Mom."

Philip: First tell me a little about Connie. Was she a religious person?

Steve: My mother had a very simple faith. You didn't have to prove to her there was a God. She didn't talk about it much; she just knew. And she could see God in every day, in everything around her.

Carmen: Steve and I met in L'Arche in France in 1972. When we came back to Canada to get married, Mom hadn't met me at all.

The first thing she said to me was "I love you." And I said, "How can you say that?" And she said, "Well, if Steve loves you, then I can, too." She was that kind of person: the fact that her son loved me was good enough for her.

P: How did she come to meet Henri?

S: We were all at Daybreak in the early eighties. Mom had retired from teaching and was secretary to Daybreak's community leader. Then she wanted to improve her French. She also wanted to find out what it was like living in a L'Arche house with the people with disabilities. So she left her job and went to live at L'Arche in Trosly in France. She ended up working as a secretary there, too, and that's how she met Henri. That was 1985–86, the year he was staying at Trosly.

C: She wrote and said, "I met this great Catholic priest, very interesting. He's Dutch and he's homosexual." Right from the start she knew that. Even though she didn't know who Henri Nouwen was—she had never read any of his books—within a week she was convinced that he was someone really special.

S: That year was an important turning point in both of their lives—Henri experiencing L'Arche, deciding to leave academia and come to live at Daybreak; and Mom realizing that as much as she liked to travel and meet people, she didn't want to be away from her family and close friends for long periods of time. So I think that was the beginning of the final stage of both of their lives, when they really decided where they wanted to be and what they wanted to do. So she came back to Daybreak, and he became pastor and she became his secretary.

Connie Ellis and Henri.

P: What did she do as his secretary?

S: At first she was doing his accounting and a good part of his correspondence. She also helped him find quality editors for his books. She would critique the manuscripts herself and say, "I'm not sure you should really be saying that," or "You should be emphasizing this."

C: She had a superb command of English. She thought he was very smart. And he thought she was very smart, too. She knew he had an important gift. She said, more or less, "I'm going to look after all the details so you can do what God has asked you to do. And that's to write and give talks." She really helped him find some space to write. When Daybreak people knocked on his door she'd say, "Let him be. He's writing now." I used to work just across from her office, and I would hear this.

He was always busy. Sometimes he would be running to his next meeting, and she would say, "Slow down, you're going to die of a heart attack." And he would say, "I'm too slim to die of a heart attack." And she'd say, "Well, then, you'll give me one!" They used to joke about it. But she really believed he would die of a heart attack.

P: What was their relationship like?

S: My mom was very much in sync with who Henri was. They had a kind of spiritual compatibility. And I think that's one thing that really attracted them to each other and made their relationship work so beautifully; they didn't have to go through any of that preliminary stuff. They were able to get to work right away.

C: But it was, I think, really more a mother-and-son relation-ship. I had an impression that Henri's mother was a bit like Con-nie. He had this beautiful photo of his mother in the office, as well as a painting that she gave him of a clown. And Mom said, "We should always have that hanging somewhere because it's from your mother."

At four o'clock they used to close the office, and they'd have their little glass of wine and their cigarettes, just like he used to do with his mom. When he was a young seminarian, he would come back home at night and have a little glass of wine with his mom and a cigarette, and they would talk about the day.

S: When he was away she kept up with the correspondence and she would send books or flowers because she knew that was what Henri wanted, so people got taken care of even in his absence. Also, Mom probably helped him adapt to community living better than he would have otherwise. He used to go over to her place to have a quiet spot to write on Wednesdays, when she was off; and she would look after him.

P: What was there for your mom in their friendship?

C: I think one thing Mom got from working with Henri was an understanding of what a complex place the world is. She was brought up in quite a sheltered world, but suddenly she was dealing with the guy on death row in the United States who'd been writing for twenty years to Henri. Suddenly she met an awful lot of people who were really suffering.

S: It was a bit like allowing a seed to grow that was already there. When she was teaching she was always most attracted to the kids who had problems. So when she had the opportunity to connect with all of these people in Henri's world, that personal ministry she'd practiced in very small ways in her other work had a chance to flower.

C: She got to know Henri's friends very quickly. So they would phone even if they knew Henri was away, because they could talk to Connie. She was able to have her own ministry to people.

Henri would hit lows sometimes, he would start to doubt himself. And Mom would say, "Don't you dare doubt yourself," just like she did with all of us. I remember Henri was invited to give a talk to an annual meeting of priests. And he said, "I will come if you let me bring some of the people with disabilities from my community with me." But "No, thank you" was the reply he got. Then Henri was having doubts about what he had done. He asked Mom, "Do you think I went a little bit too far?" And she said, "No, no. If that's what you believe, that's what you believe." Well, the next year Henri was invited again and the invitation included "Bring whoever you want." So Mom said, "I think you won that one!" There were other little moments like that, when I think Henri wanted to push the envelope, and I think Mom encouraged him.

P: Which of Henri's pastoral relationships touched her most deeply?

S: I remember she spoke about one young man who had written that he was dying alone. Nobody in his family would come near him because he had AIDS, and Henri just supported him, by phone, by letter, by visits, and by really being there when he was needed. Henri's ministry was not just celebrating the mass at the funeral. His ministry was traveling with people through their lives, being a pilgrim on the same pilgrimage, and that's what he did with Connie and us when Connie was sick and dying.

P: Can you tell me about your mother's illness?

C: In 1992 we found out she had a malignant brain tumor. There was one point after the surgery when she seemed to be giving up. Henri was away, and I thought, "God, if Henri was here, he would know what to say to her now." And then he arrived, just like that. And he just went right into the intensive care ward and disturbed everybody. "Where is she, where is she?"

S: We don't know what he said to her. Henri could reverse your way of looking at things. He presented you with another view of how you could accept the hand you'd been dealt.

C: After he left, the nurse asked me, "Who was that mad professor?" She said, "I don't know what he did to her but we've gone from 'She is going to die' to 'She's fighting.' "

S: After that she lived another two years.

One of Henri's greatest gifts was being able to talk about dying and death and grief, but that gift was for helping people not only to let go but sometimes as well to hang on. Henri wrote about this time in Mom's life in *Our Greatest Gift*. I want to read you what he said:

> *I wanted her [Connie] to believe that what was important was not only what she did or still could do for others, but also—and even more so—what she lives in her illness and how she lives it. I wanted her to come to see that, in her growing dependence, she is giving more to her grandchildren than during the times when she could bring them in her car to school, to shops, and to sports fields. I wanted her to discover that the times when she needs them are as important as the times when they need her. In fact, in her illness, she has become their real teacher. She speaks to them about her gratitude for life, her trust in God, and her hope in a life beyond death.*

C: And this was true. This is what happened. We were blessed in supporting her those two years. Our children, Sarah and Charles, helped her a lot. Not that it wasn't hard. But she was always so thankful. And before, Mom didn't really speak about her relationship with God, but now she mentioned her faith often. She was amazing.

P: And how was it at the end?

S: Mom was getting weaker and she was back in hospital. Henri was supposed to go to Germany to write, but he was anxious about being away. Maybe he sensed she was not going to live much longer. He said to Mom, "I told Carmen, 'Call and I'll come right back if there's a change.'"

C: But Mom said, "No, no. You take your time, you write. Then, when you come back, you do my funeral." They talked like that to each other. And when she went into the coma we phoned him. When he came back she was in a semi-coma. She could recognize people and move one arm, but she could not answer back. She could just mouth things. She asked him, "Why are you here?" And he said, "I think this is the end. I want to be here with you." And then she just kissed him.

Mom's skin would dry out, so I would put cream on her. Henri said, "How do you do this? Show me. I'll do it for her, too. I want to do that." And he would comb her hair, the little bit of hair she had.

S: It was Henri who helped us understand what it is to let go. The last sixteen days of her life she was in a semi-coma. We were confused: "Why is this taking so much time?" we asked. And Henri said, "Because you haven't told her that you're ready to let her go."

C: The day she passed away I told her, "It's okay. You can go now." And she died.

As for the way Henri died, Mom always said he would die of a heart attack, alone, away from Daybreak. She said he has such a close relationship with God, God will take him when they're alone together.

S: I think L'Arche gave Henri and my mom both the opportunity to live very concretely what they'd always believed about how people should live: that living for other people is more important than living for yourself.

Remembering
My Dad

TIM BRUNER

*Tim Bruner lived at L'Arche Daybreak from when he was an infant until he
was twelve. His mother, Kathy, was a member of the community, and Henri
was a good friend of the family. Now Kathy, Tim, and his younger sister,
Sarah, live in Bloomington, Indiana, where Tim is in high school.*

I was only three years old when it happened. Mum said she had
something important to tell me as I climbed up on her lap. She
said: "You know you had a daddy that you never got to meet. And
I've told you that he has been sick. Well, now I have to tell you that
your daddy has died."

"What was his name?" I asked.

"John," said Mum.

I had a daddy. His name was John. And he died.

The following spring came, and on Easter weekend Mum and
I were driving past a graveyard and at the last minute Mum turned
in. She said my dad was probably in a place like this in Australia.

The air was crisp and cold and damp. I started to run over some
freshly dug dirt, and Mum said, "Don't walk there, Timmy!" She
explained that it was a new grave, that someone had just been buried

there. Just like my dad. Buried in the ground, in the dirt. His body was in a box in the dirt, and the good part of him was with God.

Then I noticed the rock. The flat rock with all the ABCs on it. Mum said that it was a special rock, called a gravestone, and that it told about the person who had died. "Does my daddy have a rock like that?" Mum said she really didn't know. I left my mum and walked around on my own for a few minutes. I caught up with her at the car and asked if we could go to Henri's house. My pockets were full. Mum asked me what I had in my pockets. I told her that I'd found my daddy some rocks, cause she said she wasn't sure that he already had one.

Henri lived at the Dayspring. We went there a lot. Henri had always been my friend. We came to Daybreak the same year and I guess he always liked me. He came for dinner a lot, and he always was telling me funny stories about the places he'd go and the stuff he'd do there. That summer we'd even gone to the ocean together at Cape Cod with my mum. He built sand castles with me and we played in the water. He'd send me letters and call me sometimes when he was far away and just ask about my day, and he'd bring me toys and treats when he came back from trips. Henri was my friend, and I knew he'd know about the rocks. We drove straight to Henri's house.

Well, it turned out to be pretty busy there; everybody was getting ready for the Stations of the Cross service. I went straight into the chapel area and sat down next to a corner table. There was a little candle there already. I took out the picture Mum had given me. My dad, John. Then I quietly took out each of my rocks and put them around my picture of my daddy. It was a sad kind of day. But it made me feel good to do this. Henri came and sat down next to me. He asked me about the picture (he had seen it many times before) and the rocks, and he told me he really liked how I'd given my daddy a stone of his own. And when some people came over to fix the table for the next service Henri said the table was already fixed, and they listened to him. Henri told me my stones could stay there as long as I wanted them to.

Mum and I were planning to visit my uncle Kevin and aunt Gloria in Washington, D.C., in the summer. Mum said they both knew my dad, and it would be nice to be with people who had known him and loved him a lot. Mum says I started talking about seeing my dad. That when we got there he would scoop me up in his arms and hug me and tell me that he loved me. He was going to be at the zoo when we went to the zoo, and at the ocean when we went to the ocean. Mum and Henri talked together. And Henri came and asked me if we could have a really special service just for my dad. He asked me to go with Mum and find a special book that we could use to write down stories about my dad. He said it was a very special day, and that maybe it was time to visit the table in the chapel that had the waiting rocks and picture of my dad.

We found the perfect little book. I made a picture of my dad and me; it was a picture of my daddy holding my hand. Mum and I made a box, covered in white paper, and we brought beautiful candles from our house. We asked some of our closest friends to come to the chapel that day: Sue, Nathan, Elizabeth, Lorenzo, and Christiane. They were all my good friends.

Henri talked to me during the whole service. Sometimes I sat in his lap. He invited everyone to talk about my dad. My friends told me important things about my dad. They told me my daddy lives on inside me—in my curly hair! in my blue eyes! in the way we both like to read! in the way we both have loving hearts. My friends told me that I would not ever see my daddy at the zoo, or at the ocean. They told me I'd never ride on his shoulders or get a big hug and kiss from him. They all told me that they loved me very, very much. It was a pretty sad time. Then we all went outside to the garden and took my special white box. Inside the box I put my photo of my dad, and all the stones. I put in the special drawing I had made of my dad and me. Henri put in a card that showed my daddy close to God's heart. Then we closed the white box. We dug a hole in the garden, using my little shovels, and we buried the white box in the ground, in the dirt. On top of the grave we put a really large stone, and a cross and some pretty little plants that had flowers on them. Then we all held hands and said a prayer.

When we returned to the chapel Henri blessed my book and wrote my dad's name in the front: JOHN. And then he wrote:

Dear Kathy and Timmy

    It was so good to celebrate with you John's life and death and to make a little memorial for John in the Dayspring garden on April 29th, 1990. When you grow older, Timmy, I hope that you will always think of your dad with joy and peace in your heart and live out his goodness and beauty in your own life.

    Be sure that your daddy is safe in God's love and that your life is surrounded with much love of God, your Mom and all your friends, especially Henri.

Every year we celebrated the life of my dad at the chapel. Every year new and old friends joined us to talk together and remember my dad. Every year more people wrote in my little book, where they told their stories of how they knew my dad. Mum even sent my book to Australia, India, England, and the United States to gather more stories from people who had known and loved my dad. It will always be a really sad thing, to know that my dad has died. Nothing can change that. But I have been really lucky to have a friend like Henri, who loved me even when he didn't have to. He always wanted me to know how much he loved me. He loved me a lot, I know that now.

There are a lot more stories I could tell—Henri and I were together at Daybreak for many more years! I could tell you about the skits he'd drag me into at the last minute for Christmas and Easter services, or the American Thanksgiving feasts we'd eat together, and you've probably already heard about his big birthday party where he was born as a clown out of a giant egg, and his love for the circus. He was funny and crazy sometimes. And of course I know that Henri was world famous for his book writings, but I've never read any of his books. To me Henri was just a good friend. He was a friend who would refuse to eat his vegetables with me!

When Henri died it was a sad time again for me. But in a way Henri had already prepared me for what it all meant. I know how much he loved God. I'd like to think that he and my dad, John, are together sometimes, maybe even talking about me! I was very lucky to be invited to speak at Henri's funeral, doing the prayers of the faithful with Henri's good friend Fred Rogers. After the funeral Mr. Rogers said that he thought Henri had given us to each other, and we are still friends today.

Henri being born as a clown.

Henri was a big part of my life. He helped me accept what happened when my dad died and sort of filled in for a lot of things that a father would do. I thank him for that. I can only hope that people could have a person as supportive and caring as Henri in their own times of need.

ON CARE FOR
THE DYING

What a gift it is to know deeply that we are all brothers and sisters in one human family and that, different as our cultures, languages, religions, life-styles, or work may be, we are all mortal beings called to surrender our lives into the hands of a loving God. What a gift it is to feel connected with the many who have died and to discover the joy and peace that flow from that connectedness. As I experience that gift, I know in a new way what it means to care for the dying. It means to connect them with the many who are dying or who have died and to let them discover the intimate bonds that reach far beyond the boundaries of our short lives. . . . We are brothers and sisters, and our dying is truly a dying in communion with each other. . . .

Whenever we claim our gift of care and choose to embrace not only our own mortality, but also other people's, we can become a true source of healing and hope. When we have the courage to let go of our need to cure, our care can truly heal in ways far beyond our own dreams and expectations. With our gift of care, we can gently lead our dying brothers and sisters always deeper into the heart of God and God's universe.

—Our Greatest Gift

Visiting Bob's
Grave

SALLY TUCKER

Sally Tucker lives with her family in Richmond Hill, Ontario, and is a friend of the L'Arche Daybreak community. Her daughter, Lindsay, is now a university student, and her son, Mitchell, is a senior in high school. Both young people are camp counselors, and Lindsay has been a teaching assistant for developmentally challenged students.

Henri touched my family in many ways, but none more profoundly than as a friend.

I was helping Henri in his office at Daybreak while his secretary Connie Ellis was ill, and as July 2, the fifth anniversary of my husband Bob's death, grew closer, I became increasingly agitated. I had a strong desire to visit his grave, but every time the children and I had visited in the past, it had made all of us just too sad. My daughter, Lindsay, who was ten at the time, and my son, Mitchell, one year younger, no longer wanted to go to their dad's grave. Yet something in me knew that this was an important milestone in our lives.

One day I asked Henri if he would help us find a new way to

Tim Bruner, Henri, Lindsay Tucker, Paula Keleher, Sally and Mitchell Tucker.

visit Bob's grave. He enthusiastically said yes. I felt a huge sense of relief. My fear was lifted by Henri's love and eagerness to help us.

July 2 arrived, and Henri came bounding up our porch stairs and through the back door with a bouquet of small summer flowers that he plopped into a little jar of water. Lindsay had decided not to come to the cemetery with us, but Henri talked quietly with her before we left. I have no idea what he said, but her decision remained the same. Henri rooted around outside until he found a trowel, and off we went—Henri, Mitchell, and I—not reverently or quietly, but in a flurry. That was Henri!

When we arrived at the cemetery, Mitchell and I were quiet and unsure how to be. Henri showed us the way. It was a beautiful, sunny day, so we sat on the grass and Henri began to dig a small hole to put the flower jar in. We started to help a little and he asked us to tell him about Bob. Mitchell recalled that I had asked the children what they wanted inscribed on Bob's grave marker, and

Lindsay, who was just five at the time, replied without hesitation, "a kind and gentle man." So that was what the marker said.

At first it felt really strange to be talking this way, but Henri was so at home that pretty soon Mitchell was telling stories he could remember about his dad. Henri asked Mitchell, who was only four when Bob died, what his dad liked to do, and Mitchell said he liked to go fishing, sometimes alone, more often with his buddies. Henri remembered the story of a young fisherman in Holland during World War I. He had been praying all day that he would catch some fish for his family, and he was becoming anxious that he had not caught anything. All of a sudden there was a huge splash, and, presto! the boat was filled with fish. The young man had no idea that a small bomb had hit the water nearby. He was sure the fish were a blessing from God.

We laughed as he shared more stories about himself growing up. I remember Henri's gentleness with Mitchell. The time was easy for the three of us, and I knew I had found what I was so longing for—a new way of being with Bob for me and my children.

Henri told us that families in South America go together to visit the grave of a loved one. Sometimes they bring a meal to share and celebrate the life of their loved one. At first this seemed odd, but we came to be able to share an occasional meal at Bob's grave. Sometimes Mitch brings his guitar and plays from his heart. Whatever happens, we just sit together with our thoughts.

When Mitchell and I came home that day, Lindsay was curious about what had happened. Her brother was so full of brightness. He recounted the day and how much fun it had been to tell stories about Dad and to hear Henri's funny stories. Henri had even treated us to an ice cream cone on the way home! Later that day

Lindsay asked if I would take her to the cemetery. I knew that now I could lead her to the grave as Henri had led Mitchell and me.

When we go to the cemetery now there are still feelings of loss, of what would or could have been, but there is also a deep sense of gratitude for a life lived, for a man who was kind and gentle, and who is still a presence felt in our lives. Henri guided us with humor and compassion to a place not of darkness and fear but of peace. He taught us how to remember Bob in new ways, with laughter, joy, and open hearts. Now when we visit Bob's grave we remember also Henri, who was our kind and gentle friend.

Creating a Home
for Henri

PAULA KELEHER

Paula Keleher lived at L'Arche Daybreak for several years, during one of which she coordinated the Dayspring, where Henri lived and others came for retreats. In 1999, Paula returned to her native Australia to become community leader of L'Arche in Canberra.

I always knew when Henri had been in the kitchen: many more dishes than necessary had been used to make a cheese sandwich or heat a can of soup, and the dishes were in the sink as if they would be magically cleaned and put away.

I recall many funny, frustrating, privileged moments with Henri at the Dayspring as I helped it become home for him. Often I would walk into the kitchen at 7:30 A.M. to witness Henri intensely engaging in conversation with Sue Mosteller or Wendy Lywood or a friend or retreatant, perhaps about the mystery of God, or a current event somewhere in the church or the world, or the seminar or retreat he had just given, or a book he had read. It was a little deep and intense for so early in the morning, but I treasured those breakfasts because as I listened I heard so much wisdom that enriched and challenged me.

When I was asked to be responsible for the Dayspring, I felt anxious and a little intimidated. How could I possibly create a home for this man whom I had heard so much about and whose books I had read and to whom I had listened with much respect when he spoke at worship services? A man whose experiences and knowledge were so different from mine. But I discovered Henri's humanness. At home he was able to relax and joke and share about his day and ask for help with simple things. Henri and I became friends and came truly to appreciate one another.

What would always make me laugh, though, was how, promptly at 8:00 A.M., Henri would jump up, take his cup and plate to the sink, or sometimes not, fly out the door, and speed down the lane in his blue Honda to his office. In the space of half an hour I would hear such thought-provoking reflection, and then witness this child in Henri rushing off seemingly without much reflection at all. Half an hour later I would hear his footsteps again, the chapel door flung open, and Henri diving into his robes in the sacristy. Still adjusting his garments, he would welcome those who had come for the morning service and become again this calm, wise presence with an incredible gift to announce the Word.

Henri lived as though there was stop and go and nothing in between. He had not heard of going slowly. One day Henri and I were in the living room at the Dayspring talking about a new awning for the deck. There is a screen door and a sliding glass door between the living room and the deck. It was mid-afternoon and the sun was shining in through the glass. I was having a hard time describing to Henri what the new awning would look like, so I suggested we go out on the deck so I could show him. As we were moving I was half-turned to him and blinded by the sun. The glass sliding door was open but not the screen door. I walked straight into the screen door, taking it with me as I emerged on the deck.

Embarrassed, I turned around to see a stunned look on Henri's face. "How could you do that!" he asked me. Just two months before he had walked through a plate-glass window at the airport, totally shattering it. I replied, "Quite easily. I had a pro for a teacher!" We both laughed.

Henri's Greatest Gift

CHRIS GLASER

Chris Glaser is the author of seven books, including The Word Is Out *and* Coming Out as Sacrament, *the latter dedicated to Henri. He edits* Open Hands, *a quarterly magazine for congregations welcoming people regardless of sexual orientation, and is working on a daily meditation book based on Henri's life and writings. He lives in Atlanta, Georgia. Chris met Henri at Yale.*

I met Henri when I listened to a tape of his on loneliness, his first lecture for a class at Yale Divinity School in the fall of 1973. "We look for some*one* or some*thing* to take our loneliness away," he said in a thick Dutch accent. "But then we realize no *one* and no *thing* can ever take our loneliness away." He then spoke of the spiritual life transforming loneliness into creative solitude. Through his words, Henri's loneliness touched my loneliness at a time when I had moved across the country for seminary, away from family and the familiar and my first love in California.

My second encounter consisted of two handouts Henri had given the class. Ashley Montagu's *The Elephant Man* was still only a written account and had not yet been adapted for stage and screen.

And Henri's essay "The Self-Availability of the Homosexual" had just been published in a volume entitled *Is Gay Good?* The first piece spoke to me as one who had wanted to be like everyone else. Indeed, the disfigured protagonist died trying to sleep horizontally, like other people. The second spoke to my need to be myself in all circumstances. Gay people, Henri suggested, need to be themselves openly for their own emotional and spiritual health.

I dropped a church history class to sign up for Henri's course, the lectures of which became *Reaching Out: The Three Movements of the Spiritual Life.* Henri would later describe that book as the closest to his own Christian experience.

Henri was different from other faculty. He lived on campus and kept his apartment unlocked, a safe place to which everyone had a standing invitation. A student's chance remark about the many books in his office prompted Henri to remove the intimidating library. He wanted students to know that they had something to offer him despite the fact that he was so well-read. Henri offered opportunities for prayers and Eucharist both in the small prayer chapel on campus and in his own home. And he came to student events, such as the lecture given by the Reverend Troy Perry, founder of the largely gay and lesbian Universal Fellowship of Metropolitan Community Churches. Arranging this appearance by the first openly gay speaker at Yale Divinity School served as my most public "coming out."

I asked Henri what he had thought of Rev. Perry's talks. Reluctant to be critical, he said Perry had made a presentation of humor and pathos that suited the audience, mostly new to the issue. But Henri had been looking for something a little deeper. He wondered about the specifics of the spirituality that undergirded Perry's coming out, as well as the emotional complexities of a same-gender relationship in an antigay world. In retrospect, I won-

der if Henri was search-
ing for a little more in-
formation about himself.

I took Henri's gentle
criticism to heart in my
own efforts to reform the
church in its mistreat-
ment of sexual minori-
ties. My spirituality had
to come out of the closet
along with my sexuality.

My last course with
Henri was on the life and
ministry of Vincent van
Gogh. When Henri got
the idea of doing this

Henri giving Chris Glaser a cross from El Salvador.

special seminar, other professors questioned him: What ministry?
Didn't he commit suicide? But in his fellow Dutchman's paintings
Henri saw Christian compassion. Van Gogh had been a Calvinist
minister, but his solidarity with his poor parishioners got him into
trouble with the church and he was removed. After an idle period
he decided his paintings would be his sermons, offering the same
consolation the Christian religion used to provide. I think Henri
saw parallels between Vincent's life and his own; one of them was
to be known as Henri just as van Gogh signed his paintings Vincent. (Henri once wrote that the initials J. M. in the middle of his
name *should* stand for "just me.")

Though we saw each other less frequently after my graduation
from Yale, Henri's and my friendship deepened through occasional
correspondence and often chance visits. He could be a frustrating
correspondent, inviting lengthy letters, then questioning my "busy-

ness"; asking for my "feelings," then sending a brief reply promising a longer one that never came. And he was quick with advice, asked for or not. In the early years his invariable response to my difficulty establishing a long-term relationship was to ask whether I heard in this a call to celibacy. He who had taught his students that celibacy is a gift needed to be reminded that a failed relationship is not the best reason for considering celibacy.

In the early years of our friendship I believe my homosexuality was more acceptable to Henri because of my Protestantism, since Roman Catholic teaching did not apply to me. But when I started dating a priest, Henri found this problematic and not only because of a priest's vow of celibacy. He was fearful this priest would lose touch with his calling. In fact, our relationship reinforced one another's desire to serve in ministry.

The first time it dawned on me that Henri was a celebrity was during his United States tour to dissuade Americans from our governmental policies toward Central America. I saw in the newspaper that he would be speaking at a church in the Los Angeles area, where I had returned after seminary. My parents, who had met Henri at my graduation, met me there, and we sat in the balcony of a packed sanctuary that must have held a thousand listeners. The anticipation seemed almost tangible, and the excitement (marked by gasps and cries of "There he is!") when Henri suddenly appeared was akin to what happens when a rock star ascends the stage. Without notes and with his trademark flailing hands flapping like birds about to fly up to God, he delivered a dramatic, engaging speech about his experience in Central America, which he depicted as the crossbeam of a new cross on which Christ was being crucified once again.

Afterward Henri saw me across a sea of hands reaching to grasp his and thrusting books at him to sign. He waved at me and cried as if for rescue, "Don't leave till I see you!" When I finally got to him he said, "Take me to where you live and work. I want to see." It was nearly midnight by the time I took him away from the last autograph seeker. Out of earshot of his fans he said to me, exasperated, "I tell them not to have my books for sale at these events, because I get caught up signing books and I don't get to meet people."

At the time I worked in a nonordained capacity in a Presbyterian ministry of reconciliation between the church and the lesbian, gay, bisexual, and transgender community in West Hollywood, where I also lived. Henri wanted to see my neighborhood, the bars, and other places of interest. I took him first to a glitzy gay disco named Studio One. Henri looked around the large, darkened room only partially filled with dancing men and a few women at this "early" hour, lighted intermittently by strobe lights and reflected flashes from the inevitable mirrored ball of the period. He complimented the vitality of the music: "There is such a beat here!" I recalled a divinity school gathering with kegs of beer where he'd led everyone in a circle dance—once again he'd been the only faculty member present.

Then we went to a gay video bar called Revolver. Two hundred men stood drinking and looking up at monitors throughout the room that played music videos interspersed with campy vignettes from movies. Henri's eyes grew wide: "I can't believe anybody can actually enjoy this!" What he meant was, there was little interaction among the men. Their eyes were glued to the screens.

Closer to my home we cruised past an infamous hot dog place known for its drug deals. When I mentioned it to Henri, he immediately said, "Let's stop and see!" We parked and got out of the car. Henri looked searchingly at people as if he were at a zoo. He pointed to a wigged-out couple close by and asked, "Do you suppose these people are on drugs?" I easily confirmed his suspicion. His reaction was not so much judgment as wonder.

We spent a little time at my apartment getting caught up before I left him at his motel at 3:00 A.M. He returned to my home a few days later. That evening he led my weekly Bible study, to the amazement of those who came and realized who he was. I remember he mostly listened and asked a lot of questions.

Henri was always intense. That afternoon I had suggested we go for a walk along the Santa Monica coastline—my favorite place to think and pray and occasionally talk with an intimate friend. Instead he plopped himself down on my sofa and said, "Oh no, let's sit down and have a really good talk." What he failed to recognize was that the walk along the cliffs overlooking the shore might have invited a really good talk. Nothing can be so inhibiting as one conversant commanding a "really good talk."

One "really good talk" we had was walking along Henri's Speedway, as it was known to members of his community—the informal road through the property of L'Arche Daybreak. I was staying with Henri while attending an ecumenical AIDS consultation in Toronto. I told him how impressed I was by those at the gathering who were living with HIV/AIDS. I explained that I had been so open and vulnerable about my homosexuality in the church, I doubted I would want to give the church any more of myself if I were dealing with this life-threatening disease. Henri understood, yet he reminded me that the Christian's life is lived for others: thus, sharing one's illness and dying is as important as sharing other parts of one's life. Of course he would have an opportunity to do just that in *Beyond the Mirror*, reflecting on his literal brush with death.

Another revealing conversation during that visit was in a local diner. We spoke of celibacy, to which Henri felt called and committed but not without challenge. He described attending the funeral mass and burial for his uncle Anton, also a priest. After the burial, everyone went off for a little social time. People were sad, Henri recalled, but not overly. He concluded, "When I die, I would like to have someone at my grave whose life would be radically altered by my passing." In other words, Henri missed having an intimate relationship, a partner in life who would deeply grieve his loss. Of course I stated the obvious. "Henri, there are going to be thousands devastated by your death." But his readers were not what he had in mind.

During that visit I also met Adam Arnett, the Daybreak core member Henri had been asked to assist, and realized that the intimacy and tenderness expressed in their morning routine at some level met Henri's needs to be close to another human being that having a spouse or children affords others.

But it was to another member of the community—another assistant—that Henri devoted his energy in the hope of a deep emotional commitment. That man retreated, no doubt overwhelmed by Henri's need. Henri went into a deep depression that caused the community to suggest he spend some time at a place of healing. He called me several times during that period, and in my mind's eye I conjured up a bleak, wintry horizon with a low-hung cloud ceiling—perhaps a reflection of Henri's mood. Eight years later his journal from that period of heartbreak would be published as *The Inner Voice of Love*, released on the very day his heart failed him in 1996.

But in the intervening years Henri claimed more of his identity. The archetypal "wounded healer" would warn in *The Inner Voice of Love* that people can try to hook our wounded selves in order to dismiss what God, through us, is saying to them. The man who wrote that early article, "The Self-Availability of the Homosexual," was taking his own advice and choosing friends with whom he did not have to hide his hunger and his hope. Though he strongly believed in celibacy as a vocation, he enjoyed being welcomed with hugs in the homes of gay families and developing male companionships of substance.

During the last year of his life and his final sabbatical I persuaded Henri to come to Atlanta, where I had moved, to visit me and my partner. He brought flowers to our home, and I pointed out the basket of flourishing plants he had sent in celebration of my partner's and my commitment ceremony years before. I prepared a cutting board with cheeses, fruits, and breads and opened a bottle of good wine. The three of us sat on the deck of our house, overlooking a ravine with hundred-year-old trees. The next morning Henri would lead us in prayers there. That evening he took us out for dinner, and together we rented and discussed a movie that my partner had found troubling, called *The Rapture*, whose female protagonist seeks the meaning of life in a religion with a very harsh God.

Four months later Henri died. I was devastated. Not since my father's death had I felt such grief. Yet Henri continues to be an integral part of my life. *Our Greatest Gift* comforted me about Henri's own death, as he explained that the fruits of our lives are often harvested only after our timeline is complete. My mother's death prompted me to reread *In Memoriam*, about Henri's mother's death. My pain and grief at the later dissolution of my relationship made *The Inner Voice of Love* a constant source of meditation and reflection. And my sorrow at Henri's passing prompted me to lead retreats on his life and work, taking his ministry to retreat centers he had never visited and people he had never met.

As we were waiting for Henri's plane to Toronto, he had asked me, "What can I do for you? Is there anything I can do to help you?" Conscious of his fear of being exploited, yet also being quite honest, I replied, "You've already done what you can do. You came to visit us."

That was Henri's greatest gift, I believe, in his presence and his prose. He was with us.

ON COMPASSION

If there is one notion that is central to all great religions it is that of "compassion."

How is it possible to make compassion the center of our lives? As insecure, anxious, vulnerable, and mortal beings—always involved, somehow and somewhere, in the struggle for survival—competition seems to offer us a great deal of satisfaction. . . . It is clear that winning is what is most desired and most admired.

Still, Jesus says: "Be compassionate as your heavenly Father is compassionate," and throughout the centuries all great spiritual guides echo these words. Compassion—which means, literally, "to suffer with"—is the way to the truth that we are most ourselves, not when we differ from others, but when we are the same. Indeed, the main spiritual question is not, "What difference do you make?" but "What do you have in common?" It is not "excelling" but "serving" that makes us most human. It is not proving ourselves to be better than others but confessing to be just like others that is the way to healing and reconciliation.

Compassion, to be with others when and where they suffer and to willingly enter into a fellowship of the weak, is God's way to justice and peace among people. Is this possible? Yes, it is, but only when we dare to live with the radical faith that we do not have to compete for love, but that love is freely given to us by the One who calls us to compassion.

—*Here and Now*

Working with Henri

KATHY CHRISTIE

Kathy Christie was Henri's secretary for the last four years of his life. She continued as administrator for the Henri Nouwen Literary Centre into 2000, when she began a new vocation in community and family mediation. She and her husband, Jim, and their three children live in Newmarket, Ontario.

People often asked me, "How did you come to work for Henri Nouwen?" "Isn't it exciting working for someone like Henri?" "What was Henri really like?" I always felt I was disappointing them with my story. The truth is that in 1992 I responded to an advertisement in the paper. Before coming to work with Henri, I had not heard of either the L'Arche communities or Father Henri Nouwen, which was a good thing because I probably would have been intimidated by his reputation. During my interviews Henri emphasized how important it was that everyone feel extremely welcome when they made contact with him. Although Henri was quite a perfectionist in many ways, my skill levels seemed to be of less concern to him.

Working with Henri felt like home. His office was a sanctuary for him and a link to the community he loved. It was also the link to the world outside, which included many, many friends, the publishing world, conferences, retreats, and other places of involvement. I can't say that Henri was a personal friend, but we were like family in many ways. He had a deep trust in me. He also had a need to know that I was there *at all times.* He had every phone number of every conceivable place where he could contact me. One holiday my husband and I were on the East Coast when Henri sent me an SOS about a perceived problem; I ended up phoning him ship to shore as we were crossing from Maine to Nova Scotia. Talk about feeling needed! One of the few times we had a disagreement was when we had to negotiate my having "some space," but we were also able to laugh about it since Henri did realize that he was not being entirely rational in his need to have my total and immediate attention.

There was never a time when I didn't feel a part of what Henri was doing in the office or his work. I would tend to step back when he had people with him, but no. "Kassy," he would say in his accent, "come, join us." He was also very open to suggestions and changes. If he asked me for an opinion he would want my view, and if it made sense he would go with it.

Henri's inclusivity was evident in the many times he linked people he knew with each other so that they formed lasting friendships. He had a gift for bringing people together and enabling them to step over their initial caution or awkwardness so that they truly got to know each other. As soon as he hired me he urged me to get to know Connie Ellis, his former secretary, who had developed a brain tumor. This was so I could learn about the office and better understand Henri, for he and Connie had a beautiful friendship, but also so Connie could stay connected to the office "home." Connie and I became good friends, and I was part of the circle who surrounded her when she was dying. My friendship with Connie was one of Henri's gifts to me.

People would often say, "Henri seems like the absentminded professor." Not so. He was one of the most organized people I have ever met; he was thorough and had a remarkable memory for people, for details, for books, for art. And with me he was always willing to share that knowledge. This might seem surprising because he could be very preoccupied and go flying past you in the hall without even a glance of acknowledgment. But the truth was that his focus was elsewhere and he didn't see you. When Henri did connect, his full attention was there for you.

I watched Henri minister to many people; he could go to the core of an issue or problem without fear. One of his gifts was the ability to really listen. Often the people he counseled recognized what they needed but were not able to act on it. Henri's strong belief that we are the beloved of God and that God is a forgiving God freed them where they had been stuck, to ask for what they needed and to be still in order to listen to the answer. Most times people came away on a new path.

Sometimes, however, they did not. Within a short period two people with whom Henri had been communicating committed suicide; he came into the office with the weight of the world upon him. It was one of the few times that I saw all the energy drained from him, as though a part of him was also lost. But he was able to lift himself out of those periods fairly quickly (at least on the surface) in order to be with the families or partners, and he once again would dive to the center of their pain, embracing them with his care and encouraging them to share. It appeared to me that Henri had the ability to accept many things he could not change.

Henri also had an incredible capacity for joy; at birthdays or during Christmas celebrations he was like a child. He and I shared the same birthday, and whereas sometimes I would not want to draw attention to a birthday, that was not possible in Henri's presence and it was a pleasure to be part of his celebrations. In keeping with his love of celebration and his multitude of friends, the business of our local florist absolutely flourished. We were all on a first-name basis, and the florists would shudder as I faxed them lists of names for special occasions. Henri did love his friends, and strangers, too! If someone so much as said hello he gave them one of his books; I think he was his own best marketing tool.

Being with Henri during the four years I worked for him was certainly not what I would call a job; it was a way of life. Although I never brought my personal problems to him, there have been moments since he died when I would have treasured his wisdom. I believe I shared with many other people the knowledge that I could look to Henri for help if I ever needed it. When he died it felt as though a safety net had been pulled. Yet many of the things I learned from him—his love of community, his deep faith, his ability to accept things he could not change, his love of celebration, his desire to stay connected and be faithful to his friends—stay with me still, and I am grateful.

Henri answered every letter that crossed his desk in a reflective and concerned way. Regardless of storms, blizzards, or other hindrances, we would meet at eight o'clock each morning to start the correspondence before he went to celebrate the morning Eucharist. The letter here, which Henri wrote to a teenage woman who had lost a dear friend through suicide, is one of many that demonstrate his ability to be with people in their suffering. He did not know the young woman personally but had been asked by a friend if he would write to her.

Dear Jane,*

I am really happy that I can write to you simply to let you know that I feel very deeply for you, and I wish I could be of support to you at this very hard moment in your life. I know you are asking yourself why did Agnes die, why did I lose my best friend . . . why could we not prevent this from happening? . . . Even though I do not have any answers to the many why's, I still want to write to you and tell you that I am convinced that your friendship with Agnes was certainly not in vain, and the good things that existed between the two of you will not get lost, because real love and real friendship is stronger than death. Whenever two people love each other well, that love is eternal. . . .

You feel great sadness now, but I trust deeply that as you live this pain, and feel tears coming to your eyes, you can trust that Agnes' love and friendship will enter your heart more deeply and that you will find the strength to live on with the knowledge that she will continue to guide you and support you. I am sure that Agnes wants you to be a hopeful, and a very fruitful person. . . . Maybe there are places in your heart where you feel that you have not done enough for her or maybe there are places in your heart where you are angry that she left you alone. I very much understand these feelings because I have had them too when dear friends died, but I really want you to know that Agnes' death in no way is your fault, nor that she wanted to hurt you in any way by leaving you. . . .

If you would ever like to get together with me and talk, I will be very happy to do that. Feel free to call me or visit me any time you like.

With warm greetings and wishing you much hope, courage and confidence.

Henri Nouwen

---

* Identities have been changed to protect confidentiality.

ON RELATIONSHIPS

As long as people are little more than interesting characters to us, they remain opaque. We can be quite sure that
no one who is approached as an interesting character is going to reveal to us his or her secret.... Especially in the
field of the helping professions, the temptation to label
people with easy characterizations is great, since it gives us
the illusion of understanding....

Our great task is to prevent our fears from boxing our
fellow human beings into characterizations and to see
them as persons. The word *person* comes from *per-sonare*,
which means "sounding through." Our vocation in life is
to be and increasingly become persons who "sound
through" to each other a greater reality than we ourselves
fully know. As persons we sound through a love greater
than we ourselves can grasp, a truth deeper than we ourselves can articulate, and a beauty richer than we ourselves
can contain. As persons we are called to be transparent to
each other, to point far beyond our character to the true
Author of love, truth, and beauty.

—*Clowning in Rome*

Just Henri

SUSAN ZIMMERMAN

Since 1973, Susan Zimmerman has given leadership in various L'Arche communities. She also prepared the ground for the founding of L'Arche in Japan. She knew Henri as a spiritual director, a colleague and friend, and, for a time, a housemate. Susan has worked most recently in psychiatric patient advocacy in Toronto. She is a member of L'Arche Daybreak.

This is how Henri got up every morning: He did not sleep in! At six o'clock the alarm clock would ring, followed in a split second by a whack and a thud as Henri turned off the alarm and jumped out of bed. Then the closets were thrown open and in a flurry he would run down the hall and turn the icy shower on full force. He'd return to his bedroom, the cupboard doors would open and slam shut, then there would be another lusty run down the hall to a now hot shower. A minute later the taps of the sink would be turned on with gusto, teeth brushed ferociously, water splattered hither and yon. Then Henri would go back to his bedroom and dress.

By 6:10 A.M. Henri was on the phone or typing away. The day had begun. I know this because I spent four months convalescing in the bedroom between his room and the bath. Henri could not bear background noise, but Lord knows, he made his share of it!

Henri's personality was not an easy one to live with. An unstoppable whirlwind with sparks of energy flew incessantly from the core of his being. In addition, Henri was all thumbs when he left the world of ideas and entered the practicality of hands-on caregiving and daily living. He knew this. I remember him once saying, "It has always been painful to me that I am not handy."

Love is what Henri found at Daybreak: not admiration for his writing or scholarship. We loved Henri because he was just Henri. Most of us at Daybreak never read his books, some because we could not read, others because of limits on our time. Yet we knew Henri well. What more was there to read about?

My own relationship with Henri was both intimate and rocky. He directed my spiritual journey for many years. He received my private promise of celibacy and held with me and a few others this intimacy in God through silence and counsel and prayer. He carried the knowledge of my personal struggles, faults, and failures. And he advised me wisely. We also worked together for several years: he as the pastor of Daybreak and I as chair of the spiritual life committee.

Henri's genius lay in a capacity to confront the unexamined material of everyday life, the material which lies unconsciously just below the surface of our daily relationships. He confronted it first of all in himself, never ceasing to believe that all his inner struggle could be transformed when offered to others through writing. He held a nearly reckless faith that his life would bear good fruit. This faith, his pastoral gifts, but most of all his struggle and compulsive drive to make sense of his life experience and give it words is the legacy he has left to us.

A man of extraordinary courage and intellectual gifts: that is how I remember Henri. His insight could cut incisively through layers of confusion. The wisdom that resided in his heart and intelligence flowed purely through his writing into a thirsting world. His personal life, riddled with pathos and anguish, was transformed through faith and incessant labor into empathy and a deep understanding of the struggles we all have with our humanity and mortality. His tragedy: an inner turmoil like molten magma. His gift: a generosity to keep struggling, to keep integrating, to keep reflecting on what was happening within himself, for the benefit of others.

Henri with the Circus

RODLEIGH STEVENS

Rodleigh Stevens was the leader of a flying trapeze act called the Flying Rodleighs, which also included his wife, Jennie, his sister Karlene, and other troupe members—Joe, Jonathon, and later Slava, John, and Kerri. They became close friends with Henri after meeting him at a performance in 1991. The Flying Rodleighs retired in 1998, and Rodleigh and Jennie returned to their native South Africa. Susan Brown excerpted this contribution from a manuscript by Rodleigh.

We first met Henri at the Circus Barum in Freiburg, Germany, on April 16, 1991. He was staying with a friend, Franz Johna, and his wife, Reny, to work on a translation of one of his books into German, and had come to our show with his father. Our performance that afternoon touched him so deeply that he felt compelled to meet us. He returned for the evening show, secured an introduction to my sister Karlene, and arranged to join us after the show for our usual discussion of the act.

Henri immediately barraged me with questions. His need to understand what we were talking about got the better of him, and he stood in the middle of our little circle, almost blocking the talking person from the view of the others. His facial expressions were very comical, and before the end of our discussion we were all laughing at him. Henri was laughing, too.

When I finally turned the tables on him and asked about his vocation, I couldn't have been more astonished by the answer. He said, "I am a priest. I work in Canada with handicapped people and I write books." None of that seemed to me to suit this tall, balding man with thick glasses that made his sparkling eyes look larger, his constantly moving hands, big, smiling mouth, and expression of chronic confusion.

I invited him to watch our practice the next day and, to our surprise, he arrived before we did. We found him pacing around, impatiently waiting for something to happen. He had already started feeling as if he were part of our troupe.

Henri had an insatiable appetite to know more about us. It seemed that nothing was insignificant enough for him to ignore. He was bold yet sincere with his many questions, so I didn't mind telling him about the physics and engineering of the flying trapeze and about our safety. At one point I found myself defending my decision to do a high-risk routine. I also had to explain that it is not always the difficult tricks that the audience finds most appealing. Henri nodded thoughtfully and said, "You know, that is just like real life. Not everyone is impressed with who you are but rather with who you show you are."

After that visit Henri began to exchange letters with us, and in one letter he asked if he could come to see us again toward the end of the year. He gladly accepted our offer to have him live with us for a few days.

He arrived eager to see the changes we had made to the act

since he had last been with us. His mind kept jumping from thought to thought and image to image as he digested his latest impressions. That visit was the first time Henri talked about his intention to write a book about us. I told the other troupe members, and they all agreed that they would make themselves available for interviews. Henri was very pleased with our decision and I started sensing a much more serious and purposeful side to him. He had come equipped with a tape recorder and blank cassettes and seemed happy to be able to slip into his author's role.

After the first evening show there was some discord between Jonathon and Joe, and it was embarrassing to have to deal with it in Henri's presence. But he loved it. He was beginning to see that we too had our personal differences and that we made mistakes like everyone else.

Henri worked a lot on his journal and notes during that week. He explained that once he left he could not recapture the atmosphere and feelings he experienced while he was with us, and he could write with more clarity while immersed in his subject. He also went for a long walk each morning to meditate and pray. Soon Henri was well known around the circus; he often walked through the zoo and the circus folk would greet him.

I still couldn't figure out why our act engendered such deep feelings within Henri. He admitted seeing other circus shows, but he was never affected by another group of artists as he had been by us. Perhaps deep down he fantasized that he was an artist and was living out a childhood dream. Or maybe he just adopted us and the circus as his home away from home. We never thought of ourselves as an oasis for Henri, but perhaps that is what we were. I didn't read the books he gave us at the time and didn't know about his personal problems, but even if we had known more about Henri's life away from us we would still have welcomed him into our homes with open arms. He had quickly found a place in our hearts.

Henri left us at the end of that visit armed with a tremendous amount of information and our life stories to sift through, and I didn't envy him the task.

Just before we started the 1992 summer season, Henri asked if it would be possible for him to stay with us again. This time he would bring a camper van to give him some privacy and time alone to write his book. He planned to be with us for about two weeks.

The evening after Henri arrived we pulled down our rigging, hitched up our vehicles, and prepared to drive to our next performance site. We always traveled in convoy with me in front followed by Jennie driving Karlene's trailer, then Joe, then Jonathon. I asked Henri to follow Karlene's trailer. I went slowly and Henri was able to keep up fairly well. But when we arrived in the next town, I walked past his camper van and found him still clutching the steering wheel tightly, his knuckles white. I asked him how he felt, and he admitted that he never drove much, especially something so big and especially at night. By the time everyone was parked in the new circus grounds, his lights were out!

Henri was definitely "down to business" during this visit and kept his pen and pad with him all the time. I often saw him listening to our interviews and making more notes about things he needed to ask us. I had someone video the act at least once a day, and in the evenings I would go through it with Henri and explain in detail what we were doing and how it felt. He particularly enjoyed me showing him the tricks in slow motion. In fact, one time he insisted on watching the whole act in slow motion. He seemed mesmerized by the sight of the human body performing these unnatural movements and sometimes referred to what we did as a "dance in the air." By this time he had learned a whole new vocabulary from us, which he regarded as his trapeze language.

One day during that visit my mood blackened after I missed my big trick, but this didn't seem to worry Henri. I didn't care to admit my obvious failure of concentration, but after talking to Henri about it I felt better. He had that effect on us. He accepted human failure more easily than I did.

Often Henri asked us about our feelings and took a keen interest in the interactions between the troupe members. He became very interested in my role, not only as the troupe leader but also as the person to create peace if there was discord, to make important decisions for the other troupe members, and to be concerned about their private lives. Until Henri came along I had never broken my role down into all these parts, it was just my job; but Henri was fascinated that, outside the obvious physical and mental challenges we faced, we also sometimes had enormous emotional upheavals to deal with. He explained that the whole troupe relied on me for their emotional strength and willpower.

It was at about this time that Henri spoke to me more seriously about how the troupe members related to each other. He asked if there were professional jealousies or rivalries, especially between the catchers. I explained that to prevent such problems I gave no rank to any member. Even though I was the troupe leader and the one doing the complicated tricks, without a reliable catcher I would always land in the net. When we did a particularly successful performance the whole troupe received the applause.

I knew when Henri was pleased with my explanations because he would repeat them, sometimes using different phrases or words but not trying to change the meaning. He was finding all kinds of parallels and similarities to his way of life.

After this visit Henri wrote to me and said he believed he had enough material to do the book on us. He was considering making it his first attempt at a secular type of book. Later he wrote that his ideas had swung back to introducing a religious element into the book and staying in more familiar writing territory. He also told me how effective some of the parallels that he drew between the flying trapeze act and topics in his sermons were, and he was very excited about the response they were receiving.

In June 1993, Henri arrived with his friend Frank Hamilton and a Dutch photographer, Ron van den Bosch. After the finale to one afternoon show we posed for some group photos with a nice blooming tree in the background. Without him seeing, I motioned to the others to pick Henri up in our arms and support him horizontally. He just lay there like a Roman emperor being fed grapes by his servants. If he were a cat he would have purred! It turned out that Ron had made an error loading his film that session, so we had to repeat it the next day. Henri insisted that we do the "Henri in horizontal mode" photo again.

The highlight of that visit was when Henri accepted my invitation to go on the trapeze for a swing. It took him a while to get up to the pedestal board, but once there he looked like he would explode with excitement. He showed none of the fear of height that is usual for beginners; he just wanted to grab the trapeze bar and swing. I went up and put the safety belt on him and Joe kept hold of the ropes connected to the belt.

I explained what to do and reminded Henri to listen to my commands, which would ensure his safe landing in the net. He nodded in confirmation, but the silly smile on his face should have alerted me that his mind was not on the same wavelength as mine.

"Henri in horizontal mode" with Frank Hamilton, Rodleigh,
Jennie, Joe, Karlene, and Jonathon.

As he left the pedestal board his eyes seemed to grow a few sizes larger and he gasped. His reaction to my call to let go was hopelessly late, and instead of landing in a sitting position he put his feet down first and Joe had to support most of his weight in the belt before loosening the ropes. Henri was smiling so hard when he sat up that if it weren't for his ears, his lips might have touched behind his head!

In May 1994, Henri sent us his new book, *Our Greatest Gift*, which contained material from our discussions concerning trust between the flyer and the catcher. He had found a religious parallel that fit perfectly. While we were teaching him a new vocabulary, I think we were also giving Henri a new vision of his faith. Perhaps he was experimenting with these new images in his books and sermons just as we were experimenting with new routines in our act, and it may well have been just as exciting and daring for him as it was for us. Henri could identify with the passion I felt for my work because it was the same type of passion he had for writing and spiritual healing.

In early July 1995, Henri sent us a copy of the English-language version of *Angels over the Net,* the documentary his friend Bart Gavigan had filmed with us the previous Christmas. I felt uneasy at the comparison of us to angels, but later on I realized this title was figurative. The more I watched the video, the more I understood what Henri saw in us. I felt a deeper bonding with him and came to see that I had a larger responsibility in my work. I had never before thought of it as a form of community or even a form of communication with the audience.

The last time we saw Henri was in July 1996, during his sabbatical. He had met someone he thought could help him with the book about us and he seemed more sure now of its direction. He came to watch us set up our rigging and rehearse our routine. His old excitement and sense of purpose were back, and he was drinking happily from our well of community and friendship. The act Henri watched that afternoon was much different from any he had previously seen, and he noticed immediately the new combinations. (My wife, Jennie, had stopped performing because of joint pain and Kerri had taken her place.) How we had developed the new act seemed as important to Henri as the development of our friendship.

The next day I called a practice especially for Henri and offered him the opportunity to hang under John to see how it would feel to be caught. He managed to hang there for just a short time. Only afterward did I realize how much this must have meant to him, how much importance he had placed on the "catcher" in his spiritual life. I wished that just once I could have put Henri in my body to experience the exhilaration of our flight to the catcher and the celebration when we returned safely.

Also during that visit Henri attended the annual combined birthday party that Jonathon and Karlene hosted. It was the one time during the year when everyone in the circus celebrated together. Henri made the rounds with all the circus artists and musicians. Every time I looked for him he was talking to someone else. He seemed to be having a great time.

On our way to the train station in Frankfurt the next morning Henri expressed concern about some of the things he had seen at the party, and we began to feel as if he were talking to us as his own children. I enjoyed seeing this side of him. When he left we gave him a big hug and kiss on his unshaven cheek, and he looked upset at having spent so little time with us. We were sad to see him go and could only anticipate his next visit. It is now even more sad to know that this was the last time we saw our dear friend, but if we had known it then we would not have done anything differently. We would just have started missing him sooner.

After our last show on September 21, 1996, we learned from Kathy Christie that Henri had died that morning. We were stunned. Before we entered the ring the next day I made a short speech dedicating our performance to our friend Henri. I learned from Henri's family that there would be a funeral service for him on September 25 in Utrecht, a 170-mile trip from where we were. We drove to Utrecht, and when we arrived in the cathedral we were greeted like old friends by people we had never met. Henri's brother Laurent asked me to take his place as one of the pallbearers, and I could not think of a better way to make my final farewell.

I am still mystified about what moved Henri to want to write about us. I can only presume that we gave a visual dimension to his deep spiritual feelings. He made the connection between our bodies and his spirit. For instance, he compared our ability to forget about everything else in our lives during our performance with what he needed when in prayer. I think Henri's need for community was also satisfied with us. We accepted him for who and what he was. I think that we were in the right place at the right time for him, and it pleases me that we could be there for him.

Henri, we miss you. Thank you for everything you gave us, our memories and especially new friends.

ON THE
CIRCUS LIFE

It's the entertainer's life! Making people say "Ooh" and "Aaaah" and "Wow" and "Nooo"; making them feel tension and release, making them look up to the dome of the tent and say, "How can they do it? I can't believe it," and sending them home with that strange, but quickly passing sensation of having been in another world.

Is my own life very different? I travel here and there giving talks, make people feel safe or excited, and help them come to terms with their feelings of loss, failure, and anguish, as well as their feelings of growth, success, and joy. Am I—like circus people—an entertainer? Do I try to hold people up in between the many fragmented moments of their lives and give them a glimpse of "the beyond"? It fascinates me that the word *entertainment* comes from the Latin words *inter* (between) and *tenere* (to hold).

What's wrong with being an entertainer? Isn't Jesus the greatest of all entertainers? Isn't he holding people up in a life that constantly wants to go flat? Didn't Jesus come from another world and travel from place to place to let people look up for a moment and realize that there is more to life than they might have thought?

—*New Oxford Review*, June 1993

My Adopted Father

SIOBHAN KEOGH

Siobhan Keogh lived at L'Arche Daybreak in 1987, and Henri became her spiritual director at that time. She is a professional engineer who directs her own computer consulting firm. Siobhan, her husband, Kevin Bolianatz, and their daughter, Aurora, now live in Toronto and continue their friendships in L'Arche and the Ignatius Farm Community.

I came to live in the Daybreak community four months after Henri arrived. I was making the transition from the intense professional life of a General Electric engineer to the life of a L'Arche assistant. At community events I noticed people flocking to Henri. Because I came from the corporate world, where it is important to be known by influential people, I interpreted this (incorrectly) as the same power game in a new setting. I had come to learn a simpler spirituality, so I avoided Henri and focused on other members of the community. I am eternally grateful that I got over my initial reservations about spending time with him, for what a blessing our relationship has been to me!

As my year at Daybreak went on I grew to appreciate Henri more and more. Near the close of that year he offered a course on

Advent, in preparation for Christmas, and I was able to be one of the students. Henri was very good at drawing parallels between the Gospel stories and our current lives. He emphasized that the Gospel is unfolding today and that we need to live attentively and make the connections between it and our lives. We spoke of Mary's great yes to God when she learned she had been chosen to give birth to Jesus. The parallel in my life was hard for me: I felt that because I was choosing to leave Daybreak after my one-year commitment, I was saying no to God. When I made the choice to come to Daybreak, I had been so filled with joy. I felt I was finally following God. Now, though I knew that leaving Daybreak was the right decision for me, I was filled with sorrow. Henri was very attentive to my pain. He was also clear with me that leaving Daybreak was not turning away from God.

When I left Daybreak, I chose not to go back to full-time corporate life. I started my own company so that I could do technically challenging work without the long hours that had swallowed all of my life. I wanted free time to stay in contact with Daybreak, to stay in contact with the spirit. Henri helped me make the transition. He understood my different worlds. This was very important to me. When I had been a full-time assistant, people had often complained that I was "too businesslike" for L'Arche. Henri's broader knowledge helped me see my gifts and accept myself more fully. He said that he would accompany me and became my spiritual director.

Many times I was reluctant to meet with Henri because nothing profound had happened to me since our last meeting. I was still searching for the lightning bolts rather than trying to live the faithful, steadfast journey. I felt that if I didn't have deep, mystical experiences to report, I was wasting the time of the great and important Henri. (Of course, these were my feelings, not Henri's.)

Henri helped me realize that random spiritual experiences are not as fruitful as a regular spiritual discipline. I often flitted between my various activities—business, dance, church, Daybreak, travel, social justice. Henri helped me learn to commit myself. It was his encouragement (bordering on disapproval if I did not follow through) that made me commit to attending Monday night Daybreak worship services. "It is the regularity—people *knowing* that you'll be there—that's important," he explained.

Henri was always concerned with my spiritual reading. He suggested many helpful books, such as *Enduring Grace* by Carol Lee Flinders and *He Was One of Us* by Riet Poortvliet. One, *Earthy Mysticism* by William McNamara, really caught hold with me, and Henri encouraged me to read other books by the same author. He said that this was what he had done with Thomas Merton's writings. Later, Eknath Easwaran's book *Meditation* helped me develop the disciplines of daily meditation and single-mindedness. (The latter was particularly difficult as I took pride in my ability to multitask!)

Of course, Henri's interests didn't stop with books. *"Everything that you do can be done spiritually,"* he told me. "Watching a movie shouldn't end with the credits. Ask yourself, 'What does the movie say to me spiritually?' "

Not long after I left Daybreak, Henri and I were both at a Faith and Sharing retreat led by Jean Vanier. Henri shared some of the deep pain he was experiencing at the time, mainly because of rejection by a friend. I boldly asked him if he had been having a physical relationship with this man. He replied in a stern tone that he took his priestly vows very seriously and would not do such a thing. Somehow, though, my question brought us closer. For Henri it may have been because I recognized him as a sexual being. Or maybe because it let him know that his sexual orientation wouldn't

upset me. For me it was important to see that he took his commitments seriously. That question broke a lot of ice and allowed us
to enter a mutual friendship.

Our friendship intersected in the world of flowers. Henri had
a great love for art and things of beauty, and I loved the beauty of
creation visible in flowers. He often asked me to create floral
arrangements for the worship area at Dayspring and at retreats. I
enjoyed our times together making the worship space beautiful. If
someone had died, his or her favorite flowers were incorporated
into the design.

I often prayed and talked with Henri about my deep wound of
not being married. At one point, when I had been dating a particular man for a couple of months, I spoke again about this pain.
Henri's response was "What about the new man? He seems good."
His endorsement increased my interest in the man. For a year and
a half we were engaged, but the wedding was called off nine weeks
before the date.

The breakup was just part of a very dark year that included two
surgeries, diagnosis of a chronic illness, three car accidents, and the
suicide of my favorite cousin. Throughout this time Henri counseled me to continue to be faithful to God and be gentle with myself and others. I often wallowed in thoughts of the uselessness of
my life and the multitude of my faults. I was sustained by the
thought that if Henri, one of the world's leading spiritual writers,
and another friend, a leading technical writer, both enjoyed my
company, there had to be something okay within me.

Henri loved me like a daughter—a beloved daughter in whom
he was well pleased. (Well, at times.) He took great care of me.
Many have commented on his lack of homemaking skills. But over
his years at Daybreak he learned much, and I was a recipient of the
benefits of his growing knowledge. Our meetings were often over

lunch, which he would carefully present on a lovely platter. During my year of intense darkness he did a great deal for me. When he heard that my cousin had committed suicide he called me up instantly. He wanted me to come to Dayspring to rest and be in his company. I replied that I had family commitments and mourning periods to attend to. "Fine, but come up after those," he said. Though there was no empty guest room, he set up the sofa bed in the library office. Tears still well up in my eyes when I remember how graciously and tenderly he arranged my room that night, comforting me amidst my fears and tears. My mother, who has spent a great deal of time with priests and who has many priests as friends, commented, "A priest like Henri—now that's a priest!"

At some point I asked Henri if I could adopt him as my father. Though my own father was alive, our relationship was full of pain and we were not able to be present to each other for some years. Henri took time to consider the idea, then agreed. His acceptance healed some of my wounds. The "adoption" was in some ways just an acknowledgment of the reality of how our relationship had developed—his mentoring of me, our tradition of spending Christmas Eve and morning at Dayspring with other close friends, and lots of warm times together.

One Saturday evening we were sitting in his room sharing some thoughts and wine. It must have been a tough day of counseling for him, for he said: "You know, Siobhan, as a priest I get to hear from many married couples. And as the pastor here, I get to hear from many L'Arche couples. Some marriages are much better than others, but even so, I wouldn't wish any of them on you." He then lifted his glass for a toast: "Here's to being single!"

I am now joyfully married and am writing this as I begin my seventh month of pregnancy. While starting the day I told my baby that he/she was going to meet Henri Nouwen. My relationship with Henri has been an important part of my adult life and I am excited to share it with our new little one. Some may wonder how that can be because Henri has been dead for years now. But those who knew Henri also knew that he was sure relationships continue, and can become even stronger, beyond death. He knew that death often purifies a relationship. The old pains and withheld forgivenesses can fade and the purity of the love grow.

Henri's death was hard on me. Two weeks before we had spent some great time together. I had seen him for direction in the morning and then we went out for a delicious lunch. When he had his first heart attack in Holland, everything in my soul told me that he was going to die. I wanted to go to Holland to be with him. Flights were available and I had the money, but someone close to the situation discouraged me, saying, "Henri's going to be fine. He's over the worst of it now." I was very angry when that Saturday I received the news that Henri had indeed died. Especially, I was angry at myself for not believing in myself, for not following the truth of my heart. I pledged then to work hard at my spiritual growth, so as to be able to live from the spirit, open to others' wisdom but not dependent on their opinions or permission.

I was also angry at Henri. Knowing that his writings were based on the important movements of his life, I yelled at him that morning, "How are you planning to write about this, your most important transition?" The response came, "You will write about it." The "you" was plural. It would be for his friends to announce what Henri's "greatest gift" was and is in their own lives.

And what gifts have been given! The days after his death were filled with many resurrection stories—beautiful stories about forgiveness and reconciliation, love and acceptance. For instance, one woman who had felt great remorse for not thanking Henri for his kindness saw him clearly as she sang the resurrection creed, and she knew that he had risen and that he was at peace with her. There were many times when his spirit filled me. The hymn "We remember how you loved us to your death, and still we celebrate for you are with us here" touched me a lot at the time. Knowing how well Henri loved me helped me over the toughest times.

His small visits continue to warm my heart. One came on my fortieth birthday: Some people who wanted to know about Henri returned to a bookstore I frequented, hoping I would be there to tell them something about him. The salesperson said she sensed there was a deeper reason for our meeting that day. Then it dawned on me that Henri was in that moment, wanting me to know he was near me on my birthday.

The greatest gift, though, that Henri left me was a profound renewal of my spiritual life. After his death I promised to be truer to my deeper self. Henri was always suggesting that we love God "radically." (I loved how he said that word. There would be a long roll of the *r* and then enough time on the first *a* to last the length of three normal syllables.) He wanted each of us to take that leap of faith, to tear down the thin veil separating us from God's love. He also cautioned me not to be unwise, especially financially. "It doesn't make sense to give all your money to the poor and then six months later call me up needing money," he said. Many of his friends had already made these radical choices. However, I was always too cautious.

As one of the fruits of his death, I did make a somewhat radical choice. I closed my work contracts, gave up my apartment, and went off to whatever God had in store for me. What amazing blessings followed: I was welcomed by an additional community near Toronto, the Ignatius Farm Community, fell in love there, got married, and now am expecting a child. It was Henri's call to faithfulness and commitment that directly led me to meet Kevin, my husband. Kevin and I were the first couple married in the new Dayspring chapel, which Henri had put so much love and energy into planning. What a beautiful wedding gift from my adopted father! God's love is abundant, and I am deeply grateful to Henri for helping me see and realize this abundance.

Wedding of Siobhan Keogh and Kevin Bolianatz in the new Dayspring chapel.

A Continuing Presence

SHIRLEY KANE LEWIS

Shirley Lewis is the dean of Arts and Science at Aquinas College in Grand Rapids, Michigan. She and her husband, Albert, came to know Henri as a friend and spiritual guide when they spent part of a sabbatical at Daybreak. Shirley regularly brings students to Daybreak for an experience of L'Arche.

It was early morning on Monday, January 18, 1999. I had awakened from a troubled sleep filled with anxiety and memories of unmet expectations. After a lethargic breakfast I fed the dog, kissed my husband good-bye, and headed off to school. I could not arouse even the tiniest measure of excitement for the day ahead. I felt leaden and tired. It was still pitch dark as I touched the remote control to open the garage door. I knew I could not get through the day alone. I needed Henri Nouwen's spirit at my side. As the garage door opened fully the North Star appeared, brighter than usual. I asked Henri to stay by me throughout the day, and I knew he was there. The star was so luminous I felt its presence even inside the garage. I called the star Henri. As I drove to my college a profound relief washed over me. I felt like this all day and consequently had one of my most memorable and peaceful days at work.

Henri Nouwen had and still has a tremendous effect on my life. I came to Daybreak with the notion that my secular degrees, experience, and ability to hide my pain would make me invaluable to the members of the community. I was strong and stoic. The only one privy to my secret, vulnerable side was my husband. Henri helped me to change the ways I saw myself and to accept the person I am. Like an archer hitting a bull's-eye, he helped me to identify my pain and embrace it rather than shun it as I had done all my life.

I see him before me as if it were yesterday. Minutes after my husband, Albert, and I first arrived to live and work at Daybreak for a couple of weeks, Henri was sprinting down the hall to welcome us. Grinning, his hair askew, his very thin torso enclosed in a worn-out crewneck sweater, with his huge hands he waved us toward him. What struck me most were Henri's hands. They resembled the enormous hands of the statue of St. Mark in Venice, which enfold the Bible.

Henri took us under his wing for our stay. We talked every day, sometimes for a few minutes, sometimes for an hour. We had dinner with him several times. We shared wine and conversation almost every night. One evening in particular I talked with Henri for nearly two hours about the fears of rejection and abandonment that had been so much a part of my childhood. We shared our feelings about the euphemistically named "dark places" we crawl into when we are frightened. This disheveled, compassionate priest knew himself what I was talking about. He validated my dark place and in turn validated me.

Henri also taught me how to pray, so that my words to God would facilitate freedom in my soul. He taught me to spend time with myself each day, to meditate or just be silent. Silence is not natural for me; I am drawn to noise and commotion like a moth to a flame. But today, in my prayers, Henri is always right up there, listening to and supporting me.

The last time I spoke with Henri was when my father was very ill in the spring of 1996. He called me with great concern and compassion in his voice. We chatted for a few minutes and then, after thanking him for calling, I said, "I love you, Henri. Please take care of yourself." He said that he loved me too and that we would see each other soon.

It seemed significant that Henri died immediately before Yom Kippur, the Day of Atonement, the most holy day in the Jewish calendar, a day of fasting and seeking forgiveness. One important part of the day is a special memorial service for those who have died. The physical reality of Henri's death was harder for me to accept than that of my own father. I could barely imagine a world without him. But I didn't have to; he is still very present.

Broken Sunflowers

ALBERT MICHAH LEWIS

Albert Lewis is the rabbi emeritus of Congregation Emanuel in Grand Rapids, Michigan, where he served for twenty-eight years. He is recognized for his interfaith and race relations work and his liturgical and homiletic writings. Albert and his wife, Shirley, met Henri when they spent part of a sabbatical at Daybreak. They return for visits and to lead retreat days.

In the mid-1980s, while developing an academic program in gerontology, I was invited to watch a video in which Dr. Henri Nouwen talked about aging. I had never heard of the man but, eager to learn as much as I could, I came to see the video. My first impression was that this was a disorganized but enthusiastic lecturer who had little to offer me. Within a few minutes, though—fascinated with Henri's openness and depth—I became convinced that I wanted to know more about him.

The next day I asked a friend, a Roman Catholic nun, if she had ever heard of Henri Nouwen. "Of course," she replied. "We were all required to read his *Wounded Healer*." Within a day I had obtained *The Wounded Healer*, and I instantly became a reader of Henri. I knew that it was important for me to meet this man and learn

more from him, not about gerontology but about spirituality—
and about myself. My comfort in the Catholic and Jewish communities as well as my desire to learn from masters outside my own
tradition drew me closer and closer to Henri. But it would be another ten years before we would meet.

In January 1995 at Henri's invitation, my wife, Shirley, and I spent
the first two weeks of our sabbatical at L'Arche Daybreak. Soon after we arrived I observed an expression of male intimacy that I
might easily have missed. My teachers were both males and longtime members of the community. Roy Turkel was eighty years old
and Lloyd Kerman was seventy-two. They met almost daily with
other seniors—men and women. The program for seniors is held
in a Daybreak home and members are encouraged to simply be.
"Being" implies being oneself, being part of the community, and
being able to say what's on your heart, with care for the other.

On this day the seniors had invited me to morning tea. While
we were enjoying our tea and biscuits, Roy looked up at Lloyd—
who was sitting across the room—and said loudly: "Lloyd, you're
a jackass!"

Lloyd sat for several seconds, then responded from somewhere
in his apparently congested chest: "And what are you?"

Roy now awaited his allotted seconds and then said: "A bum!"

Again Lloyd waited, as though rehearsing the words of this
carefully scripted and choreographed exchange, and said: "And
what else?"

"A jackass!" exclaimed Roy.

This was followed by deep laughter and radiant smiles from
both men.

No other words were exchanged between Roy and Lloyd for the

next hour. Neither was particularly talkative. If asked questions that could be answered with a yes or a no, they would respond. Otherwise they would remain silent, taking occasional catnaps throughout the morning. It was clear that there was turmoil and words and experiences in their heads, but part of their disability was the inability to express themselves in commonly understood ways. And yet, as I listened to Roy and Lloyd over the next several days, their ritualized dialogue took on a richer meaning. It was, to my mind, a shared communication of love, respect, and profound gratitude for one another. And they invited everyone in the room into their special warmth.

The exchange between Roy and Lloyd affected my sense of being for the remainder of my time at Daybreak. In truly life-altering ways, this intimacy unfettered some of my own guardedness and led me into a wonderfully intimate relationship of my own.

Part of the self I brought to Daybreak was a man who for most of my adult life had struggled with issues of intimacy, especially with men. True intimacy among men, I have learned, requires an acceptance of vulnerability. Only in the past few years, after considerable therapy and risk taking, can I draw close to another man and say: "I want to really know you, and I want you to know the real me. I want to be able to laugh with you and cry with you . . . and not hear about it two weeks from now!"

I now have five men friends who understand my need for intimacy and who share their own hunger with me. I arrange to have lunch or dinner with one of my intimates almost weekly. I talk about my work, frustrations as a writer, and family conflicts. I question my effectiveness as a rabbi and try to talk about my fears. I do not expect my friends to be my therapists. From each of them I expect a caring ear, a sharing heart, and a great sense of humor.

During the two weeks Shirley and I spent at Daybreak, I knew that I wanted to draw closer to certain individuals, one of whom was Henri. He had kindly welcomed us into his home at the Dayspring. He had been encouraging about my proposed book and was very sensitive to my presence at daily mass. Indeed, he had invited me to comment on certain Scripture readings, which, he realized with chagrin, conveyed a distortion of Judaism. My being a Jew and a rabbi clearly called forth Henri's sense of ecumenism and hospitality. Had he not been somewhat settled about my Jewishness, he would not have invited my wife and me to stay at Daybreak, and certainly not in his own home. I believe that Henri knew I shared his journey toward a deeper intimacy with God, and that we might journey together, perhaps on parallel paths.

I began to realize that I wanted more than breakfasts with Henri, a special blessing at each mass, and dinners out together. I wanted, deeply needed, to place my heart in Henri's massive hands, to explore it with him, to show him the places of my pain. I wanted Henri J. M. Nouwen to know the hurt and fear beneath the veneer of his guest and fellow traveler. And I was able to say: "Henri, I want time to talk with you . . . just the two of us."

He responded immediately: "How about later this afternoon?"

When we sat down together, I said, "Henri, I hurt and I am angry and frustrated. I need your help and insights." Into his trustworthy hands I placed feelings from fifty years of overachievement and underappreciation. I am the eldest son. I am my colleagues' confidant. My parents never call. My congregation takes, but wants more and more. I confessed having felt impotent and inadequate, even when a small voice within told me otherwise. And he listened. I knew, in the same way that I would later understand how my brokenness is my strength and my imperfection is a blessing and not a curse, that he had heard these words before—when they were his.

An hour and a half later Henri challenged me to remain open, and he shared parts of his pain and journey with me. He told me, as his own sadness seeped from his eyes, how he had filled the classrooms at Harvard, published and lectured widely—and been denied tenure. He too had experienced significant achievement and deep disappointment.

At last a calming silence filled the small room, and each of us basked in it. We hugged and looked deeply into one another's eyes. Through a shared vulnerability, we had become one with the One.

A few days later Henri celebrated his sixty-third birthday and Shirley and I were among the guests. A poem was my gift to him then. I had come to L'Arche prepared to write prose. Instead, poetry came forth.

To my friend, Henri

O my beloved Henri,
When your arms extend
Like eagle's wings
I am borne aloft
Among all the souls
That have ever been
That ever will be,
And I am one
And you are one—
As God intended
One and one are one with the One.

You have blessed me
With your hands
With your words

With your eyes.
You are the priest
In the sanctuary
Of my soul's sadness,
The Aaronide* who
Heals the harshness
Hurled against my hungry heart.

In the light you share
From within
You told me
Every sunflower in van Gogh's vase
Is broken
Each is flawed.
Together they become whole
Petal by petal
Stem by stem
One flower at a time
All under the translucent wings
Of the ONE
Who gently glides
On the breath of life.

Wonderful friend,
I carry you
In my healing heart;
In my prayers
Your name remains.

---

*Aaron was the first priest of the ancient Israelites, called by God and anointed by Moses.

I would not see Henri again after that visit. Though I returned to Daybreak, it was when Henri was away lecturing. We spoke a few times by phone, occasionally exchanged writings, and looked forward to our next time together. On the day before Yom Kippur, the Day of Atonement, of 1996, we were called about Henri's sudden death. At the beginning of the Yom Kippur service, with the synagogue filled with worshipers seeking individual and communal atonement, I told my congregation of nearly six hundred people that my dear friend and mentor Father Henri Nouwen had died and that I was in mourning. Those who knew of my profound respect for Henri's work and of my love for Henri himself mourned with me. They knew that it was as if I had lost a family member.

Recently, I listened to Henri's taped workshop on the prodigal son. As I heard his voice again and recalled his passion, I wept for all I had lost and all I had gained.

Wonderful friend,
I carry you
In my healing heart;
In my prayers
Your name remains.

The Men's Group Camping Trip

CARL MACMILLAN

Carl MacMillan came to L'Arche Daybreak from Boston, where he did grad-
uate studies in management at Brandeis University and was for several years
an advocate for people with disabilities. At Daybreak, Carl worked closely
with Henri developing the Dayspring. He continues to live in a Daybreak
home and serve on the community's leadership team.

In 1991 a small circle of men who were in or close to the Daybreak community formed a group. We were an eclectic bunch: our
work lives diverse; some single, some married with children; our
range of affect from boisterous to subdued. Yet we also held much
in common. We were all in or approaching the broad band of middle age, drawn to a spiritual path, each eager to explore his journey
in friendship with other men. This was the era of Robert Bly's *Iron
John*, and men's groups were, if not common, at least "cool." Henri
was a part of this group, and unless he was away he met with us
once a month until the time of his death.

Every summer we would go on a weekend canoe outing. I remember well the first trip. Henri was not a seasoned camper but he
was thrilled to be going. We knew that with his schedule all we

Henri and Carl MacMillan in Algonquin Park.

could reasonably ask was that he show up. He did, wearing his "uniform": a light blue oxford-cloth shirt with a button-down collar, gray polyester pants, black shoes. He had packed his suitcase along with his briefcase, which was about the size of a small suitcase. Over his uniform he had on his London Fog trench coat. Henri was ready to go camping. We grinned and welcomed him aboard the minivan. When we reached Algonquin Park, a vast provincial park in northern Ontario, we unloaded our canoes: one for two, the other for three. Henri settled into the middle of the three-man canoe, offering the occasional paddle and being the moderator of conversation. Henri loved to talk, about almost anything.

As soon as we unloaded at the first portage, Henri found his suitcase and his briefcase. From the suitcase he unabashedly withdrew the handle that allowed him to wheel it—through the forest. After about two minutes we heard him call, "Where are we going?" "Gate 7, Henri," one of us yelled back.

After we arrived on our island and set up camp, we could relax. It was a sunny day. Campsites were far apart. No motorboats. Rarely a person in view. Wild men that we were, we all skinny-dipped.

In his briefcase Henri had brought his chalice, his Bible, and all the essentials for the Eucharist, the table of communion. Henri celebrated the Eucharist every day, and our island was a magnificent open-air chapel. We read and listened to the readings, sang (softly and uproariously), and reflected on the Scriptures together. We prayed candidly for our own needs and in gratitude for each other. Then we gathered around the communion table—a tree stump or a rock or the top of an overturned canoe. One by one we took the bread and drank the wine. This was Henri's contribution to the weekend: to bring us together in ritual as men who were weak, vulnerable, and yearning for communion.

ON CHOOSING
OUR FRIENDS

The spiritual life is one of constant choices. One of the most important choices is the choice of the people with whom we develop close intimate relationships. We have only a limited amount of time in our lives. With whom do we spend it and how?

Sometimes we act as though we will be lucky if there is anyone who wants to be our friend. But that is a very passive and even fatalistic attitude. . . . As people who trust in God's love, we must have the courage and the confidence to say to someone through whom God's love becomes visible to us: "I would like to get to know you, I would like to spend time with you. I would like to develop a friendship with you. What about you?"

There will be no's, there will be the pain of rejection. But when we determine to avoid all no's and all rejections, we will never create the milieu where we can grow stronger and deepen in love. God became human for us to make divine love tangible. That is what incarnation is all about. That incarnation not only happened long ago, but it continues to happen for those who trust that God will give us the friends we need. But the choice is ours!

—*Here and Now*

Uncle Henri

MARC VAN CAMPEN

*Marc van Campen, the second eldest of Henri's six nieces and nephews, was
the recipient of the letters Henri later published as* Letters to Marc about
Jesus. *He and his wife, Marije, and their daughter, Sterre, live in Amsterdam. Marc practices tax and venture capital law, and Marije is a communications manager for a human resources service.*

Although he was not often in the Netherlands, Uncle Henri clearly
cared much about us, his nieces and nephews. And he was the one
to make sure that our tradition of Christmas together was upheld
after his mother, our grandma, died in 1977. Christmas was the
fixed family gathering for the Nouwens in Geysteren, the home of
my grandparents. Henri would lead a mass for the family, sometimes in our grandfather's church, sometimes in the intimacy of my
grandparents' home. He also ensured that between the children's
play and the adults' business discussions we made ourselves conscious of all the good things we had and took time to think about
others. For us as small children this was difficult to understand.
But Henri always tried to talk to us and hear how we felt and
thought.

Henri was keen to add to our development, to give us something extra as we matured, to help us become good people. He surely would have liked to have us closer so he could have seen us grow in character and personality. When he was in the Netherlands he always had many people to see, so he tried to use his rare moments with us well. At dinner he would try to catch up on the news of his sister and two brothers and other adult family members, but as well he always would ask us about developments in school and about our friends and sports. He would also tell us about his adventures (so they seemed to us) in the United States, in Central and South America, and throughout Europe.

Henri decided to invite each of us to spend a summer with him when we were about fifteen years old. He considered that age old enough to appreciate new experiences and young enough to be open-minded toward different values and ways of life. I went in 1984, when Henri was in Cambridge, Massachusetts, just when I was going into my fourth year of high school. There were constant opportunities for observing, absorbing, reflecting on, and reconciling the many new experiences I had that summer with my existing framework. I spent six weeks at the summer program of a prep school with a hundred seventeen-year-old kids from New Hampshire. Henri popped over every now and then, and for two weeks I traveled with him, meeting his friends, seeing his places.

This was the first occasion that I spent considerable time with Henri in one stretch and we got to know each other better. This was also when Henri started to discuss religion with me. My immediate family did not practice religion in any significant way, though I knew what was in the Bible and we went to church once in a while—with our grandparents, for instance. Henri did not push religion on me. But because it was such an essential part of his life, I did get some idea of what it meant for him and the people around him. I discovered that religion for Henri and his friends was much less about a formula for being a "good Christian" than I had thought. He made me see that it was a way of life, not distinct from our ordinary lives.

That summer made me think about life and see it as more than a sequence of events that just happened to occur. It was a very important step in my growth into young adulthood. It broadened my horizons geographically and, especially, intellectually. Henri was right: this was a good age for such an experience.

At the same time Henri's life seemed odd to me. It was socially rich, with many people who admired and loved him. He shared very intense moments with friends, and his relationships had a depth that my relationships rarely reach even now. Still, it seemed lonely—always traveling, always arriving or leaving—and he seemed to lack a home. I remember being struck by Henri's lifestyle. He did not care for anything material; he could not recall what clothes he wore the day before; he would forget to eat. These elements were unimportant to him. He was busy with people, communicating his thoughts as much as possible. He had no interest in the expense of travel and telephone calls, seeing these as means to communicate more of his thoughts to more people. This was quite astonishing to me because I had been brought up to be aware of the cost of things.

To me Henri seemed somewhat the weird professor who did not have an eye for the real world but lived in a different world. However, he did connect with people in the real world, and people meant everything to him. For Henri, giving meaning to his life and finding happiness were inextricably linked to the people around him. The more frequent and intense the interpersonal contact, the better. The only way that Henri could stay in one place and not see others was to write books, another way he could pass on his ideas to people.

After our time together in the United States, Henri encouraged me to keep thinking about life, to see that it is not just about survival or success, that there is an extra dimension to our lives that is bigger, that gives meaning. He had found this dimension through his Christian belief, but he was conscious that this did not have to be the same for others. He made me realize that the rituals and do's and don'ts are just a first step in understanding what religion means. Religion is not just about being a good person and living life so as to go to heaven. No, Henri taught me that the characteristics I had identified with religion are just the outer circle. What really matters is a fundamental attitude of seeking to do something that is valuable to yourself and to the world. What I learned from him—and this changed my views about religion—was to think about what I would regard as a really important achievement. He also pointed out that many of the core values of anyone's life can be found in the Bible, that these values are universal. People could find meaning in other religions or in something other than religion, such as a certain philosophy or ideology. Henri emphasized that keeping my eyes open for such higher goals was what was important.

When I was eighteen a lot of Henri's message was hard for me to grasp, and even harder to pursue in spirit. In the Netherlands religion was much less openly discussed than in the United States, and expressing yourself on this subject was regarded as abnormal or silly. This was one of the reasons why Henri did not feel at home in the Netherlands. When he was there he could not discuss the subject that was most important to him and constantly on his mind.

But having a somewhat regular challenge from Henri did make me think about my life and take the first steps toward discovery of that extra dimension. I talked to certain friends about this process and tried to give it a place in my life. (I am still finding my way in this regard.) Henri's life and writings provide helpful material for this search, which he pursued so intensely himself.

My introduction to Henri as a writer came with the book that was published in English as *Letters to Marc about Jesus*. Henri had thus far written all his books in English, and when he was asked to write a book in Dutch he proposed to write letters to me. I was still just eighteen but was happy to take on the role of recipient. I thought that it would help me find some of that meaning in life that Henri had explained to me and convinced me was worth searching for. I would try to understand what Henri was telling me and give it a place in my life so that it shaped my values and ideals.

So Henri started writing and I started reading. I usually spent quite a while on each letter before I felt that I had gotten the gist of it. At the time I thought that this was part of being new to the subject. Afterwards, others indicated that Henri's letters are pretty tough reading material for most young people.

Henri's letters were always linked to something that he had seen or that had happened in daily life. This made what he wrote about much easier to relate to and apply to my daily life. One letter focused on the events in the Philippines, where President Ferdinand Marcos was overthrown without bloodshed by the party of Corazon Aquino. In this example he showed me very clearly that loving someone is easy if that person is always being good to you; but really loving someone means that if that person (Marcos in this case) is not good, you still treat him or her with love. Then your love becomes truly meaningful. My wife, Marije, and I chose to share parts of this chapter at our wedding mass in 1997. We wanted to emphasize to our guests how love can manifest its strength.

Because the letters that Henri wrote were so challenging to me, I regularly met with a small group of friends to discuss them. But since not everyone was open to this kind of conversation, I selected these friends with Father Rabou, the priest of the church I had started visiting since my return from my summer with Henri. Father Rabou was like Henri—very much aware of the value of the core or the essence of the Christian religion, and not one to emphasize the form and appearance generally associated with the Roman Catholic Church. We discussed the letters one by one. Often it took quite some time before everyone grasped the meaning of a letter. Then we talked about how we could actually use the letters in our lives.

One of our general feelings was that these letters were written with Jesus and the meaning of life as the focus, but we could read all of Henri's letters as examples of how to become a better religious or nonreligious person, not just a better Catholic or a better Christian. Henri did not restrict himself to Christian examples. This was also why Father Rabou was enthusiastic about the letters: they could provide everyone, Catholic or not, with help to think about values in life.

Also, we all thought that taking the message to heart was one thing, but actually changing our lifestyles in accordance with those ideals demands a great deal more. We realized that daily life presented us with opportunities to be giving to others, to kneel down rather than to elbow our way up, to love despite being hit in the face, even though our instinctive reaction is to choose our own interests over the interests of others. To actively stick to those ideals and take another route is hard.

After I went to university in Amsterdam and met Marije, the

Dutch secular life got the best of me, and my contact with Henri slightly diminished. But he was one of the first to ask me whether I intended to marry Marije, and if so when. It could not be soon enough in his eyes. Unfortunately it took us until 1997, less than a year after his death, to decide on marriage. Now we have a daughter, and it is up to me and Marije to give little Sterre some of the ideas, some of the values that Henri lived and that he passed on to me, to us, to many.

Henri and My Bat Mitzvah

ELLEN WEINSTEIN

Ellen Weinstein came to L'Arche Daybreak in 1978. In 1994, at age thirty-five, she celebrated her Bat Mitzvah (literally, "daughter of the commandments"), the Jewish coming-of-age ceremony for a young woman. Ellen works at the Woodery and continues to attend synagogue services regularly. She asked Beth Porter to help her tell this story.

Beth: What did you do when you decided you wanted to have a Bat Mitzvah celebration?

Ellen: Talked to Henri—in his office. Told him I want a Bat Mitzvah. He was happy.

Rabbi Troster visited. I welcomed him. So did Henri.... I practiced. With a tape. With Toni, Susie, other people. We had dinner at Lieba's house. She's at the synagogue. My mom and dad came. Shalom, because he reads the Torah. Henri, Toni, Paula, Joe, you. Henri said to me: "Why are we having this dinner, Ellen?" And I said, "Because I'm having a Bat Mitzvah." I had to decide who should do different things. I chose my dad and Henri to talk. I said Mel Kirzner to hold the Torah, my aunt and uncle to have a part. I chose *The Giving Tree* to read.

B: How did Daybreak people learn about your Bat Mitzvah?

E: Well, Henri said, "Come to Dayspring." Henri talked about my Bat Mitzvah. I practiced the blessings. Everybody prayed for me. I said to everybody, "Are you coming to my Bat Mitzvah?"

For my Bat Mitzvah, I got a *tallit* (prayer shawl). Henri talked to me in front of everybody. He said I'm a Jewish woman at Day-

Ellen holding the Torah scroll.

break and that's important. People danced. They didn't forget the candies. We had a big lunch with cake. Yumm! Lots of people from Daybreak came. I was very happy.

I always will remember Ellen's Bat Mitzvah on a very blessed event not only in Ellen's life, but also in the life of the Daybreak Community. More than ever we learned about the love for the Torah.

Henri

Henri's note in Ellen's Bat Mitzvah album.

ON TALENTS
AND GIFTS

It is worthwhile making a distinction between talents and gifts. More important than our talents are our gifts. We may have only a few talents, but we have many gifts. Our gifts are the many ways in which we express our humanity. They are part of who we are: friendship, kindness, patience, joy, peace, forgiveness, gentleness, love, hope, trust, and many others. These are the true gifts we have to offer to each other.

Somehow I have known this for a long time, especially through my personal experience of the enormous healing power of these gifts. But since my coming to live in a community with mentally handicapped people, I have rediscovered this simple truth. Few, if any, of those people have talents they can boast of. Few are able to make contributions to our society that allow them to earn money, compete on the open market or win awards. But how splendid are their gifts!

—*Life of the Beloved*

Lessons in
Openness

BETH PORTER

Beth Porter has lived at L'Arche Daybreak since 1981. Before coming to Daybreak she taught college English for several years. She knew Henri as a friend and colleague. Beth chairs the interfaith committee of the community's pastoral team, writes on spirituality and interfaith matters, and helps in the Daybreak Seniors' Club.

One of Henri's most striking qualities was his openness: he was not threatened by new ideas and challenging situations that might cause others apprehension. Rather, they seemed to awaken his creative energy. In L'Arche Daybreak the effect of this openness was broadening. For me it took two forms: Henri's introduction of his friends and his pastoral concerns and interests outside the Daybreak community opened my mind and heart to situations that had previously seemed alien or distant, and his encouragement to study theology gave new intellectual and vocational direction to my life.

Henri did not keep his friends to himself when they came to Daybreak. He was eager that they know us and that we know them and their work. Through our contact with these people of diverse backgrounds, engaged in varied and often quite radical ministries, we became linked into the remarkable network of faith and hope that Henri facilitated.

In the 1980s, when the frightening extent of the AIDS epidemic in North America had become evident, and alarm—and judgmentalism—in the general population was high, we were receiving visits from people who daily gave physical care and spiritual support to people with AIDS—frontline workers like Mary Carney, Michael Harank, and Chris Glaser. Then Henri spoke at a major AIDS conference in Chicago. He returned to share with us the suffering and courage of those he'd met there. Influenced by Henri's compassionate concern, I became more aware of both the discrimination faced by people who were gay and the great hardships under which people with AIDS, gay or not, lived. I found myself shedding prejudice I barely knew I had held.

When Henri's friend Father John Vesey visited from Guatemala, we sat spellbound as he recounted the martyrdom of his predecessor, Stan Rother, in the parish of Santiago Atitlán and the struggles of the oppressed and terrorized people there. He told us of his efforts to support their cottage weaving industry, and the continuing threats with which he lived. Three years earlier Henri had visited John and, with the photographer Peter Weiskel, had written *Love in a Fearful Land*, the story of Stan and John in Guatemala. I conceived a great respect for Henri's willingness to risk by going there, by writing that book, and by speaking publicly in ways that challenged American complicity in the civil strife in Central America. I knew that Henri had a healthy curiosity and enthusiasm for new experiences. He was not reckless, but I realized that he would venture into risky situations for reasons of faith and friendship.

I was always struck by Henri's attraction to what was just and right. Most often his Dayspring homilies were directed to helping us live well together and receive the gift of God's presence in our day-to-day relationships, but for Henri it was axiomatic to support strongly all who worked for justice, and help them live rooted in a deep sense of their safety in God. He invited to our liturgies visitors who worked with homeless people in downtown Toronto and asked them to speak. In prayer he would mention his friends in the U.S. peace and justice movement, some of whom were in prison. Always he modeled a compassionate attentiveness.

One public encounter became a paradigm for me. At a crowded interfaith trialogue at the University of Toronto, an older Jewish woman in the front row, her voice full of emotion, lit into Henri as a representative of Christianity, which had so failed the Jewish people during the Holocaust. The room fell completely silent. Henri listened thoughtfully, crouching so he could make eye contact; then, speaking directly to her, he validated her challenge, acknowledging the history and expressing his sorrow for the failures of the Christian Church. I was impressed by his honest and empathetic response, and I thanked God he did not react defensively or try to insert stories about what the church or Christians did do for the Jews. This interaction made an especially strong impression on me because I was, at the time, becoming much more aware of the history of Jewish-Christian relations, particularly of the devastating effects of centuries of Christian theological anti-Judaism.

I had by then begun studying, partly because Henri had influenced Daybreak to support members who wanted to pursue new endeavors. He pointed out that having some assistants involved in academic life could benefit the whole community, and he recognized that I needed intellectual stimulation and a change of emphasis. He urged me not just to take a few courses but to pursue a degree in which I would be able to wrestle with theological questions and receive a good pastoral education.

Henri helped me plan my field education at Daybreak. He proposed that I practice giving short reflections at community worship services and offered me helpful feedback. Himself the consummate journal writer, he asked me to keep a journal and form a theological reflection group with whom I could share my writings. He was focused on what this would do for others in the community as well as for me. Henri was a part of this lively, synergetic group, and the experience taught all of us the life-giving possibilities of reflecting together theologically on the daily interactions of L'Arche. Henri had a gift for listening and contributing in just the right way to help the dynamism.

When I expressed a desire to learn about modern Jewish issues, Henri urged me to take courses offered in Israel and he largely financed this part of my studies. Also, he introduced me to the writings of Elie Wiesel and Abraham Joshua Heschel, whose books he had brought to Daybreak in his personal library, and he spoke about his experience as a young priest assisting his uncle Anton Ramselaar at the Second Vatican Council. There, Henri's uncle had lent theological support to a reform of the Catholic Church's teaching about Judaism and the Jewish people.

Henri encouraged me to share what I was learning about Jewish-Christian relations in ways that changed and deepened our Daybreak liturgical life. On Holy Thursday, at the celebration of Jesus' institution of the Eucharist, he asked me to speak about the roots of the Eucharist in Passover and Jewish table fellowship. In early Advent, Henri, Mary Bastedo, and I were having lunch together when I lamented the problematic references to Israel in the ancient and much-loved Advent hymn "O Come, O Come, Emmanuel." "Of course, in the hymn the church understands itself to be Israel, but that is just the problem," I remarked, "the appropriation of the Jewish people's name and religion, and without even an acknowledgment." Then I feared I had thrown a wet blanket on our conversation. But Henri immediately affirmed my comment and shifted us to brainstorming for a more satisfactory wording. Thanks to Mary's musical gifts, within a few minutes we had come up with a revision that continues to be sung at Daybreak.

When I started taking my Daybreak friend Ellen Weinstein to a synagogue Henri was supportive, and when she decided she wanted a Bat Mitzvah (the Jewish coming-of-age ritual for a woman) he was enthusiastic. "We will put her celebration at the center of the community," he said. "We don't want it happening over on the side. We can all be enriched by this." He outlined a series of weekly announcements and plans for two common worship services at which Ellen would speak about her preparation and the community could pray with and for her. On the day of her Bat Mitzvah members of the synagogue and Daybreak came together around Ellen in joyful festivities that led to an ongoing relationship between our communities.

Henri also encouraged my efforts to enable Alia Qureshi, another Daybreak core member friend, to connect with her Muslim faith community and help us learn more about her faith and traditions. When we invited Alia's father to speak to us about the Muslim holy month of Ramadan, Henri was present, listening attentively and thanking him warmly. It was Lent, and in subsequent homilies Henri referred to the richness of the spirituality of fasting in Islam and to how Mr. Qureshi's sharing had enabled him to think about fasting as in itself a form of prayer and an avenue to communion with God.

In time my primary focus became the search for an articulation of Christian theology that would allow a respectful space for religious pluralism. When my studies took me intellectually and spiritually into territory outside traditional theological formulations, Henri continued to journey with me.

My most future-oriented theological discussion with Henri occurred after I mentioned, half sadly and half excitedly, that I was having great difficulty relating to traditional Christian language and doctrinal expression and felt alienated from my faith, but I had been reading some process theology and could see a possible complementarity between it and the new physics. We didn't pursue the subject at the time and Henri soon left on a trip. But when he returned he immediately insisted that we have lunch.

We were barely seated when he launched into a discussion of ideas from quantum physics and how they might provide us with language to describe God. While he was away Henri had had a conversation that led him to build on my earlier comment. We began exploring process theology. Did it necessitate jettisoning the idea of the personal nature of God? This, we agreed, was key. Almost everything else could be seen as metaphor that could be replaced with new metaphor. Perhaps we needed to think in terms of God as more rather than less personal than we can imagine, or perhaps as suprapersonal. Could we think along the lines suggested by writers in the Jewish renewal movement, such as Michael Lerner— of God as the force that makes possible transcendence and transformation?

Pooling our limited knowledge of current physics, we marveled over the continuous, unperceived interchange between matter and energy, the constant movement and shift in state of subatomic particles, and the posited multidimensionality of reality. Recently some scientists had suggested that there are at least ten or twelve dimensions, even though we humans perceive only three, four if time is included. I shared the intriguing comment of the sixteenth-century Jewish mystic Isaac Luria that God must have contracted God's Self to allow space for creation. Were the unperceived dimensions God, or God's dwelling place?

I was surprised that Henri seemed as excited as I as we talked of reimagining Ultimate Reality—an unsettling proposition if one's faith depended strongly on familiar metaphors. We reflected on how the language of religion helps us express our faith but is not absolute. While Henri used the well-known stories and images of Christian spirituality in his talks, he was no literalist, and he was much too sophisticated to confuse metaphors with the reality that is beyond all language. I experienced in him an expectation that God is ever greater than and further beyond both our perception and the linguistic formulations to which we are accustomed, yet is always intimately present.

When I finished my master of divinity degree and was reentering the daily life of Daybreak, wondering how best to use my education, Henri participated in my clearness meeting, a Quaker tradition designed to help a person decide on a course of action. Out of this meeting came, in time, a mandate from the Daybreak Council to continue my interfaith work as part of my role as a community member. It is work I do with joy and with much gratitude to Henri, who in his exemplary openness recognized, welcomed, and affirmed this vocation within my vocation to L'Arche.

How Big Is God?

MICHAEL CHRISTENSEN
AND REBECCA LAIRD

Michael Christensen directs the Doctor of Ministry Program at Drew University in Madison, New Jersey. He came to know Henri as teacher and friend at Yale, and often lectures on Henri's spirituality. Rebecca Laird, an author and speaker, edits Sacred Journey, *the journal of Fellowship in Prayer, in Princeton, New Jersey.*

"Guess who's coming to dinner?" In July 1996, in response to an invitation to lead a retreat for Drew University faculty and students, Henri informed us by fax that he was on a writing sabbatical at the guest house of a friend "not far from you." No, he wasn't taking any speaking engagements this year, but he'd love to have dinner with us.

Henri arrived for dinner with flowers in hand. Our then three-and-a-half-year-old daughter Megan was soon in Henri's lap, asking him to read her a book. Six-year-old Rachel told him that she had seen his picture in the book lying on the coffee table.

We reviewed the last decade and a half of life and ministry over dinner, good wine, and coffee. Soon to turn sixty-five, Henri said he wanted to devote as much time as possible to writing and pastoral work. He no longer wanted to fly here and there to meet important people, but to spend time with close friends and embrace the life of prayer, community, and ministry.

After dessert we settled in to watch the opening ceremony of the 1996 Olympic Games. Henri huddled with us around a tiny television screen with Megan on his lap. During a commercial break, she asked, "How big is God?" Henri replied, "God is as big as your heart." Megan continued to probe: "And how big is that?" Henri smiled and gestured with his large hands. "Your heart is big enough to contain the whole world."

A good answer, repeated often in our household, especially since Henri's death. Requiring romantic language and paradoxical images, it may baffle academics, but it engages three-and-a-half-year-olds—it's a mystic's vision.

Remembering
Henri

JOHN F. DOS SANTOS

John dos Santos is professor emeritus of psychology at the University of Notre Dame in South Bend, Indiana. He was a population adviser for the Ford Foundation in Mexico in the early 1980s. From 1957 to 1965 he directed research programs at the Menninger Foundation, the influential psychiatric institute in Topeka, Kansas. He and his wife, Mary Alice, and their family knew Henri in all of these settings.

I first met Henri in 1964, when he came to the Menninger Foundation as a fellow in the religion and psychiatry program. I remember him as enthusiastic, friendly, and interesting. He soon became deeply absorbed in all he was learning in the stimulating intellectual atmosphere of the foundation. During this time a small group of Roman Catholic professionals met monthly in our homes to discuss religion and its relationship to our lives and to therapy, psychology, and psychiatry. Henri was the youngest and least experienced member of the group and generally said less than the others, but it was clear that his time at the foundation was very important to his personal and professional development. He became a family friend, and Mary Alice and I would invite him to dinner both for our five children, who had immediately fallen in love with him, and for our own enjoyment of his company.

Shortly after I went to the University of Notre Dame in 1965 to establish the Department of Psychology and its graduate program, I asked Henri if he would be interested in coming to South Bend as a faculty member. He agreed but expressed some concern about his lack of academic experience and the challenges for him of working in an American institution. My decision to invite Henri into the department was based on his different educational and cultural background and his promise as a mentor, counselor, and teacher. I also thought that I could trust him to be an honest and realistic adviser as I developed a psychology program in a Roman Catholic university that was still not entirely comfortable with the discipline.

Indeed, about such issues Henri proved to be quite open-minded and practical. But he tended to be much more reticent about strictly academic and departmental matters. From its inception the department was strongly oriented toward scientific psychology and research. I suspect that this emphasis made Henri feel somewhat marginal and uncomfortable. He wanted to be better informed about our research on perception and cognition, so another faculty member and I discussed conceptualization, research design and methodology, statistical analysis of results, and hypothesis testing with him. He was very interested and attentive but quickly realized that this was not the sort of study he wanted to pursue. Soon afterward he became more involved with pastoral theology.

In his first semester in the psychology department I assigned Henri to teach an undergraduate offering in personality development. He worked hard to organize and prepare the course, and it proved quite popular. A number of his students became devoted admirers and he often ended up as their personal counselor and confidant.

As Henri became more involved with the development of pastoral theology at Notre Dame, his academic connection to the psychology department diminished and then ended. Our contacts became largely social; we had dinner together and celebrated special events with visitors or his parents and other family members.

After Henri left Notre Dame in 1968 we saw him only sporadically until 1982, when I was working in Mexico City and Henri stayed with us while he studied Spanish in Cuernavaca. Upon his arrival we learned that, in a typical Henri gesture, he had given his clothes and money to someone who "needed them." So Mary Alice took him to purchase new clothes and get enough money for his stay.

During this time Henri encountered some everyday situations that challenged his belief in the basic goodness of human beings. For instance, he tended to pay cabdrivers and vendors with large bills and then fail to count his change on the spot. He would come into the house counting and recounting his change, searching and re-searching his pockets, only to find that he had been badly cheated. He just couldn't believe that some vendors and cabdrivers would do such a thing. Of course, since Roman collars and religious garb were not allowed in public, people didn't know that they had stolen from a priest. But it may not have made any difference to them.

On a trip to Guatemala and Costa Rica with Mary Alice and me, Henri truly enjoyed mingling with the crowds and shopping in the markets. However, bargaining he could not do. In Guatemala City he wanted to purchase some beautiful handwoven stoles that he later used as vestments in saying mass. But he became upset about my persistence regarding the asking price because he was concerned that we would deprive the clerk of his just profits. I suspect Henri never believed me when I told him that such bargaining was expected and respected, and that it was almost certain that the clerk worked for someone else who owned many booths in the market and paid very low wages.

When Henri left Mexico for Central and South America, we found ourselves involved in some frantic, last-minute preparations. Unfortunately, on our arrival at the airport in Mexico City we discovered that Henri had lost the document he needed in order to leave the country. I had to convince the airline agent that Henri was a Dutch priest, an associate of Cardinal Alfrink, and that he was on an important mission for the church in Central and South America. This was, to be sure, a somewhat expanded version of the truth, but the agent was sufficiently impressed that he allowed us to look for the duplicate of Henri's document in the airport's records room.

Then came what I have always referred to as Henri's miracle. The records room was about the size of a basketball court and filled with tables stacked with two-foot-high piles of tourist cards. I told Henri that this would be a ridiculous, futile search, with untold thousands of cards to check and a plane scheduled to leave in a few minutes. However, since there was no other choice, we approached one of the tables, where Henri picked up about five cards from a stack and, without any obvious surprise, said to me, "Here it is." I checked the card, looked up to the heavens, and thought, "You never do anything like this for me!"

During Henri's later occasional visits to South Bend it became difficult to see him because of his many commitments. Every now and then, though, we would hear from him as he moved from place to place. Over all the time my family and I knew Henri, he remained, with us, pretty much like the energetic, interested, friendly person we first knew at the Menninger Foundation. He never talked with us about his personal pain. Certainly our fondness for Henri makes it difficult even now to think of the suffering and despair he lived with at times in the last decades of his life.

The news of Henri's death brought our family great sadness and revived memories of the times we had spent with him. Above all we remembered his love of beauty in people, artwork, flowers, and architecture. He once spoke eloquently about how much he appreciated having beautiful things in his room and in his life. He was distressed by lack of beauty, even in homes, buildings, and cities. As he put it in his own unique style, "Too often they are just plain ugly." How ironic that such a kind, gentle, and beauty-loving soul had to face so many just plain ugly personal demons in his much too short life.

From August 1964 to December 1966, I was a student at the Menninger Foundation. . . . They were the most formative years of my life as a student. The Saturday Colloquia with Dr. Karl [Menninger] will always remain one of my most precious memories. During that time I so enjoyed the support and friendship of Tom Klink, Paul Pruyser, Dr. [Herman] Van der Waals and his wife, Seward Hiltner, Ken Mitchell, Richard Bollinger, and John and Mary Alice Santos. It was John Santos who brought me to Notre Dame.*

---

*Henri's inscription in his copy of Lawrence J. Friedman, *Menninger: The Family and the Clinic* (Alfred A. Knopf, 1990).

A Map for Life

JACK STROH

Jack Stroh and his wife, Sue, live in Erie, Pennsylvania, where Sue has served on the board of the Erie L'Arche community. Jack is recently retired from practicing business law. Earlier in his career he served as a trial attorney and an instructor of military justice in the U.S. Navy, and as a civilian litigator. His professional life was transformed by Henri's spiritual guidance.

By the end of the 1980s, I had become very disillusioned with the practice of law. Since 1965 I had been working in a highly competitive environment, and in my law firm partners even competed against each other. I had gradually come to believe that I had complete control of my life: if I kept my competitive edge honed and went on working longer and harder, I would always be successful. And if I wore a Teflon suit that deflected any criticism, my family would understand, would still love me, and everything would be fine.

But it wasn't exactly working out that way. Losing a case here and there, finding out that my clients didn't always tell me the straight story, and learning that hard work wasn't necessarily the way to win began to exact their toll. So I turned to more competition—marathon running, marathon cross-country skiing, marathon biking. Drinking was becoming a problem, and my weight was going up. When I gave up alcohol altogether—a startling change—I lost friends. I was thinking of quitting law, selling everything, and going somewhere to serve God, but I had no real plan. Very alarming to my good wife, Sue.

I *was* ready to do something else, but I was also in fact very depressed. Sue asked me if I would be willing to talk to a man she had met through L'Arche, a man called Henri. If she had asked me to go see a priest, I'm sure I would have refused, but she presented him as "this interesting and nice man" (who just happened to be a priest). So without thinking it through, as my lifetime training required, I said yes.

It was Sunday afternoon when we got to L'Arche Daybreak in Richmond Hill. I had come straight from a legal conference in New York that taught ways to work harder and smarter and make more money from the unsuspecting. It served to highlight the growing conflict between my experience practicing law and my essential humanity.

Henri was most welcoming and warm. In no time I was describing to him the way my professional career was spiraling out of control and my need for some ideas on how I could reorder my life. I told him that on the drive up I had had to pull off the road frequently to match Sue's written directions with our road map. "Henri, I need to pull off my own road now, to check my directions, and I need someone to give me a map." Immediately he responded, "I will do that"—no hesitation, utter confidence, complete certainty.

Henri began the process of guiding me at our first meeting by simply giving me a pocket-sized monthly missal. He asked me to try to read the designated passages each day. Before long I told Sue, "Hey, there's some pretty good stuff in there; maybe you'd like to read it, too." Later I said, "Let's go to the mass and hear all the words and what the priest has to say about them."

During that first weekend Henri also gave me a copy of his book *In the Name of Jesus*, about Jesus' temptations in the desert—to be relevant, to be popular, and to acquire power—and Jesus' re-

Jack Stroh and Henri.

sponses to those temptations, which are models for our responses to these same temptations. It was as if the words were directed to me. I was to seek solitude (the desert), to be silent (to listen), and to pray always.

Over the next few years Henri, Sue, and I developed a little routine: At least once every three months I would leave my office early on Friday and we would meander along the byways to Daybreak, stay overnight in the Dayspring, just "be" all day Saturday and Sunday morning, and leave after Henri's eleven o'clock mass at St. Mary Immaculate in Richmond Hill to meander back to Erie.

Friday night always began with dinner followed by the community Eucharist. As Henri's houseguests we were treated royally. However, Henri would continue his own schedule, which at times could be very crowded with visits, meetings, and telephone calls. Saturday morning would usually start with morning prayer in the chapel followed by toast and coffee in the kitchen. Many times Sue and I would do grocery shopping or get things Henri needed for his next trip, and Sue would cook supper on Saturday night for the three of us and occasional guests. If Henri wasn't too busy we might go out to dinner—he particularly liked Chinese food—and then we would just relax, reading and talking.

We never did have a fixed schedule for the weekend. We always made sure that Henri and I would have some time to talk privately, but the only "fixing" we did was by the end of one visit to have the next firmly scheduled. Sometimes we talked for long periods, many times informally at meals, over an evening glass of wine, or just "in between" other events, exchanging even as little as a sentence or two, which would later become a subject of conversation. Other times we were more formal, in Henri's office-bedroom in the Dayspring.

I often told Henri, and I think he agreed, that simply being with him was all I really needed. I found so many things to be seen, heard, felt, and learned just by being around Henri and his many friends and visitors. And, oh, what I learned.

I learned that I really am the beloved. God knew me, knew my name, from all eternity and called me to be here now. I learned that Christ really did come to call sinners, and I, as a sinner, was being called, directly and by name. And so, my heroes from history came to be those who had things on their records that needed to be forgiven, and when they were, went on to become some of our greatest leaders and teachers—King David, St. Paul, and St. Augustine.

I have changed dramatically. I wasn't knocked off my horse like St. Paul, but I did play on the railroad tracks—the high-speed line of competition, control, relevance, applause, and power—too long and got hit by the train. Henri quietly and gradually nursed my transition process. He said he would give me a map and he did.

Henri first struck a responsive chord with me when he told me about his father, Laurent. Laurent was a tax lawyer but he was also a teacher and certainly not the mean-spirited hired gun we are so familiar with in the United States. Henri through his father showed me that there were better, more integrative ways of practicing law; that there was indeed a way out for me other than walking away from my firm and putting on sackcloth. As Henri later pointed out, and it came to pass—I was sitting on my own ministry, where my life and history could lead and teach others. I could, like his father, guide clients and partners to the *right* result, known in their own hearts to be best even when it meant giving up some power, control, money, revenge, prestige, or other short-range advantage. So now, when presenting a client with options, I'm not afraid to ask, "Which choice is best for your life now? Which will let you sleep well at night for having done the right thing?"

In a way, Henri's talking about this holistic approach to practicing law and my adoption of it were prophetic. Today in the United States there is a movement in the legal profession toward this approach.

Henri also led me to others who changed from being "of" this world to merely being "in" it: Charles de Foucauld, Thomas Merton, Arsenius, and the other desert fathers and mothers. I saw that my salvation also lies in regularly seeking solitude and prayer. Henri put us in touch with the Camaldolese Monastery in Big Sur, California. There, with the monks who were so fond of Henri, Sue and I continue to spend times of quiet and spiritual nourishment.

When Henri first showed us his icons, of which he was so proud, I expressed interest so he offered to lend us one during Lent. Of course, we picked Henri's favorite, the Pantocrator, Christ with his hand raised in blessing. He had acquired it in Jerusalem. But, trusting soul that he was, he let us take it back to the States. He explained how we could set up a prayer table in our home. We did so, and the red vigil light became a matter of some discussion in our neighborhood. We were most encouraged, however, by the Jewish family across the street, who said that it was an inspiration for them despite the difference in our religions. We now have our own icon and pray with it every Lent and every Advent.

When Henri died, I lost the person who had so regularly given me teaching words that could penetrate to the very core of my heart. I recognized those words as God's own and that he was using Henri to bring me to where I could know and love my Lord.

At first I thought I would have to reread all of what Henri had written and said. But it turned out that was not necessary. Oh, I do reread Henri, but I found that what I learned from him and through him has become part of my own existence. So now when I am called to speak, I find myself saying things that I know Henri would say, not in his style but in my own manner. When I am called upon to act or not to act, I find myself responding according to this new understanding in my heart, which brings me to the correct action.

In my law firm I find myself consciously refusing to judge people's words or actions. I actively look for the Christ in everyone. I look for the gifts and talents that each one brings to me, my partners, and our business. In 1997 I was elected to the management committee, and later I completed a two-year term as managing partner, from which position I was able to change the way some people, including some of my colleagues, think about and practice law.

I realize how important it is to forgive. To treat everyone as I want to be treated. We need to forgive unconditionally and then let things go. And when it happens again, forgive again. But I also learned the need to accept forgiveness. That's why I admire Paul and David and Augustine so much. They were men of the world who made mistakes but accepted God's forgiveness and got on with life. Once you're forgiven and accept it, you can do so much. You're truly free. Unforgiveness lets us write other people off, or write ourselves off! I see this close up in the law profession; lawyers hold things against each other or their clients for years. But forgiving and being forgiven has brought a new fruitfulness to my work life, and there's a sense of blessing in my family life as well.

My relationship with Henri continues to this day in a most powerful although different way. Like Henri, I have come to recognize both the prodigal son and his older brother in me. And I've come to recognize my duty to become an earthly father, to try to show everyone I can the loving, eternal embrace that awaits us all. St. Francis de Sales, patron of writers, whose feast day is January 24, Henri's birthday, said, "To love someone in the highest sense of the word is to wish that person the eternal possession of God and lead him to it." This is what Henri did for me, and what both Sue and I want to pass on to others.

A DISCIPLINE OF
THE HEART

The spiritual life demands a discipline of the heart. Discipline is the mark of a disciple of Jesus. That doesn't mean, however, making things difficult for yourself, but making available the inner space where God can touch you with an all-transforming love. We human beings are so faint-hearted that we have a lot of trouble leaving an empty space empty. We like to fill it all up with ideas, plans, duties, tasks, and activities.

It strikes me increasingly just how hard-pressed people are nowadays. It's as though they're tearing about from one emergency to another. Never solitary, never still, never really free but always busy about something that just can't wait. You get the impression that amid this hurly-burly, we lose touch with life itself. We have the experience of being busy while nothing really seems to happen. The more agitated we are, and the more compacted our lives become, the more difficult it is to keep a space where God can let something truly new take place.

The discipline of the heart helps us to let God into our hearts so that God can become known to us there, in the deepest recesses of our own being. This is not so easy to do; we like to be master in our own house and don't want to admit that our house is God's house too.

—*Letters to Marc about Jesus*

My Search
for Henri

MICHAEL FORD

Michael Ford is the author of Wounded Prophet, *a portrait of Henri published in 1999 and since translated into several languages. A journalist for the British Broadcasting Corporation, he has a home in Somerset, England, where he keeps his own Henri Nouwen library. In this contribution Michael describes how Henri's life unfolded for him through his research.*

One gloriously warm September afternoon I was strolling around the peaceful village of Trosly in France, talking with members of the L'Arche community about the extraordinary life and times of Henri Jozef Machiel Nouwen. I was wondering how the restless, company-loving writer had coped with the silence of the place when someone suddenly said something that made me stop in my tracks: "Henri was either in the oratory or in the phone box." It was an off-the-cuff observation that seemed to cradle a deep truth about the person I was writing about—a man who naturally spanned two worlds.

A similar scenario unfolded when I spent a weekend in Rotterdam with Henri's brother Laurent and his wife, Heiltjen. "When Henri came to stay, he was on the phone for so long that nobody could reach us," they told me. "We were cut off, so we had to have another line put in just for him." They also pointed out that no matter how long Henri had been on the telephone the previous night, he would always be up at six to say the divine office.

As I tried to keep up with Henri's footsteps around the world, his faithfulness to prayer and his fidelity to the telephone featured frequently in the conversations. I'm not certain if there were toy handsets in the 1930s, but if so Henri must surely have had one somewhere in his playpen. Even after suffering a heart attack in the last week of his life he managed to persuade the nurses to fix up a telephone jack next to his hospital bed so he could dial around the globe.

Henri spent a lifetime helping people connect with God and one another. *Connecting* might be a term normally associated with the telecommunications industry, but for Henri it was a profoundly spiritual concept that underlay much of his theological thinking. In his writings he was always at pains to connect one idea with the next, even though at first glance there might seem to be little in common between them. Henri also linked unlikely people and diverse communities in ways that sometimes astounded those who knew him. The Latin word for priest, *pontifex*, means bridge-builder: the priest is the person who builds a bridge between humanity and God. Through his zest for divine and human communication, Henri paved the way for his readers and friends to experience the presence of God in their lives. To me, he was first and foremost a priest for all people.

Henri also had something of the journalistic temperament within him: restless, always in a hurry, inquisitive, fascinated by people and the way they relate, determined to write down his experiences and get them published. It was, however, his own inner life that became the subject of his most extensive reportage. Some found his style too self-absorbed for its own good, even narcissistic, but many others were able to make connections between Nouwen's own psychospiritual life and their own.

Digging into the life of your spiritual hero is an unnerving affair, especially when you have no idea what to expect and wonder if you will be disappointed. What I found was that Henri was undoubtedly a person of utter sincerity who would never deny the questionable things about himself. But the "real" Nouwen, as described by his friends, was somewhat different from the individual who emerges in his books. He wrote about many of the issues with which he struggled, and he tended to give the impression that it was all under control. It wasn't. This was partly because his autobiographical style was sometimes rather contrived and partly because readers were often inclined to overlook those faults and failings to which he owned up in his books. At the other extreme, because his texts were more stilted than he ever was, they had the effect of disguising his natural ebullience. Those accustomed to his qualities of abundance did not always recognize the spiritual leader portrayed in the writings.

I had always been fascinated by Henri's life. The first time we met, I pressed him on his influences. "I don't have any," he replied. "I love art and I love conversations." Sensing, I suspect, a touch of idolization, he pierced my illusions by telling me that he was really "a very ambitious person." I didn't give credence to his words until the research I was doing for my book revealed a man striving for success and popularity. His inclination to veer toward the limelight and engineer situations to suit his own needs hardly seemed compatible with the man I thought I knew. He was not the introvert his books suggested, and yet, for all his dramatic extroversion, he still struck me as a humble man of endearing contradictions.

What emerged clearly from my research was that Henri had been "a saint with wounds," as one person put it. He had given so much and he had suffered so much. Pain had fueled his creativity. God had worked with and through his struggles to give people hope on their own spiritual journeys.

It was also enlightening to discover that, throughout his life, Henri seemed to have managed to "do his own thing," especially in the institutions where he had studied and worked. Few priests of his era can have been as successful in carving out such an individual path. He discerned that he had been given a unique prophetic gift which could never have found adequate expression had he become a parish priest, bishop, or conventional academic. His was a spirituality that paradoxically owed as much to his own autonomy as it did to struggle and self-questioning. He sought opportunities to test his vocation and live out his restlessness. Each new experience became the vehicle for another book. And if he couldn't live the life with which he was experimenting, he would write honestly about his difficulties and then turn in another manuscript. For example, while he was at the Abbey of the Genesee he kept a journal, and this became *The Genesee Diary*. Henri might well have felt attracted to monastic life, but I sense his reporting instincts came more naturally. He became instead what he was best suited for—an arch between spiritual theology and popular writing.

He was also a bridge between Roman Catholicism and other branches of the Christian faith and, without becoming political, brought people together in ways that no other spiritual leader of his generation had. His writings moved Orthodox Christians, Catholics, Anglicans, and Evangelicals as well as readers from other faiths. While this testified to his ecumenical and interfaith vision, it was never an indication that his own beliefs were being compromised or diluted. Embracing the worlds of theology, psychology, and journalism, he cut through the religious red tape to reclaim the spiritual life for the priesthood of all believers.

It was a unique accomplishment, but it was achieved partly, it must be said, because of his fears about not being loved. He was always living up to other people's expectations of him, and it wore him out. His success had made him a household name, but it also fostered circumspection. And it was probably for this reason that he dared only hint at his sexual orientation in his writings. Henri knew of spiritual writers who had been deserted by their readers when it became known they were gay.

But Henri was not frightened of perfecting a style of writing which connected his own insecurities with those of his readers. What was ever in evidence was his ability to draw masterfully on his psychological experience and understanding in crafting his spiritual classics. I still consider him a prodigious figure in the world of contemporary spirituality, but my hope is that people will now examine his work more critically in the light of his own life story.

For all the flexibility of his ministry Henri never achieved the inner liberty he desired. Little wonder that he was drawn back time and again to the image of the flying trapeze. As I watched the Flying Rodleighs rehearse one cold December afternoon on the outskirts of Frankfurt, their act came to symbolize all that my research was teaching me: that Henri secretly yearned for the freedom to be himself. The trapeze became the embodied symbol of the Christian life, centered on letting go and being caught. Living and dying was about trusting the catcher and becoming the person

God intended you to be—body, mind, and soul. Through these theological insights Henri came to discover more about the vulnerability and joy of human relationships.

When I finished *Wounded Prophet*, I hoped it might go some way to explaining the "real" Henri Nouwen without dispelling the mystery. But it is not the last word on him, nor is it intended to be. Others will see him through different shafts of light. In an inscription to a book he once sent me, Henri wrote: "Grateful for your friendship and your willingness to let me be part of your adventurous journey with God." I can only return the compliment.

Sowing in Tears, Reaping in Joy

ALAN AND JUDY STEERS

Alan and Judy Steers held various roles at L'Arche Daybreak over several years, and their children, Emily and William, were born there. They now live in the Niagara region of Ontario, where Alan, who has since been ordained to the priesthood, serves an Anglican (Episcopal) parish and Judy is a professional youth minister and musician.

The wedding day had arrived! The Dayspring chapel was decorated, friends and family were gathering, a banquet had been prepared by a loving cousin. People had come from near and far: assistants and core members from the L'Arche Daybreak community, relatives and friends from across Ontario, family from England and Scotland.

Deep within myself, though, I knew I was not ready to marry Judy. I had awoken early to pray and prepare, but I was overwhelmed by an enormous uneasiness. My brother, staying at the apartment with me, tried to assure me that it was just a case of wedding nerves. But I knew that it was much deeper than that. I needed to seek out some spiritual guidance—no, a spiritual lifeline—as I saw my dreams shattering before me, consumed by a deep, inner conviction that all was not right.

It was nine in the morning. I knew Henri had just finished celebrating Eucharist at the Dayspring chapel. For five years I had known Henri as my pastor in Daybreak, where I lived as an assistant. I'd worked as a colleague with him on our spiritual life committee and had come to love and trust him as a friend and guide. One of his greatest gifts was the ability to put words to our experience and then show us how God might be seeing that same experience "from above." That was a phrase he often used—so much so that many people thought he might one day write a book about it!

We were friends, too. I had a special place in Henri's circle in that I was deemed one of his best mimics. When Henri had been at Daybreak five years, Jean Vanier and others came to help him reflect upon his experience. The intense three-day evaluation ended with an uproarious festival; bishops and benefactors, brothers and sisters enjoyed skits and send-ups. The climax of the event was my impersonation of Henri giving a lecture on five "pillars of the spiritual life": Hoomility, Entoosiasm, Noorrturing, Rraationality, and Inspirration (H.E.N.R.I. for short!).

But that drizzly, midsummer morning of August 1994, I had a much heavier heart. I knew it was Henri I needed to talk to. I went to find Judy. She was quiet, deeply concerned, yet, to my surprise and relief, understanding. She put the decision back to me: "You decide. I'm not going to get angry and force you into something to which you are not committed."

JUDY: What could I say? Nothing prepares one for moments in life like this. I was surprised that I was not angry. Nor despairing. I had a strong sense of this moment being very *real* and deeply human. In a most anguishing way, something was being called forth from me. The situation was at once unbelievable and totally honest. But what would everyone else say? I wondered. Nobody cancels their wedding on *the day* of the wedding! Part of what enabled me to walk with Alan at this moment was the memory of my first brief, failed marriage nine years before. I had known on my wedding day that it hadn't been right. But who can actually acknowledge those terrifying feelings? And who can support another person through a moment of such extreme vulnerability, or give support to make such a countercultural decision? I encouraged Alan to talk with Henri.

I found Henri in his office. He was preparing to go to Ukraine the next day and was frantically busy. I went to another room to wait for him and he came to me. He listened, taking my doubts and fears seriously. He reassured me of God's love, of Judy's love, of his love, and he hugged me. "Now it is up to you to decide. I will come back at twelve." The wedding was set for 3:00 P.M.

At noon I returned to find Henri. I was in anguish and complete turmoil and no longer knew what to think or do. Judy arrived and, misty-eyed, asked me, "So, are we getting married?" My tear-filled eyes met hers and I quietly said, "I don't think so." Henri spoke: "Whether you get married tomorrow, next week, next year, or never, it is clear that you are not in a position to make a good decision today. And, you know, you don't have to get married today!" With alarming clarity I recalled Henri's words from our marriage preparation, spoken most forcefully two months before: "If you are not ready to get married, then no matter how much money has been spent on the wedding, no matter how far people have flown to attend, no matter that everyone is all dressed up, you don't have to proceed."

The wedding was off. I called my family. Judy and I, with broken hearts, looked to Henri and asked, "What do we do now?" We felt empty, wounded, and ashamed. We both had a sense of wanting to run away and hide. Then, in words that neither I nor Judy will ever forget, Henri said, "Now, we go together to the chapel, where all your family and friends are waiting for you. All the people who most love you. We will celebrate the Eucharist together." Astonished, we replied, "You're kidding." "No," continued Henri, "today you are broken and vulnerable before your friends and community. What better time to celebrate the Eucharist, the feast of Jesus' solidarity with all who are broken and in pain, the feast of the broken body?" We trusted our friend and pastor but were also too stunned and exhausted to argue!

At the Dayspring thirty-five people were gathered for the intimate service we'd planned. Not everyone had heard there was to be no wedding. We were seated in a circle as was the practice there. We could see who was in pain, who was angry, who was confused, and who was just watching events unfold. Henri spoke first: "You are welcome here. . . . Judy and Alan have decided they are not getting married today. . . . Here are two good people listening to the deepest convictions of their hearts; that is, they cannot get married. They are calling you, their family and friends, to live this deepest moment with them." People began to relax. Judy's father, having heard the news an hour before, later related that this was the moment he stopped having heart palpitations and began to breathe easily.

Our friend Nathan Ball, Daybreak's community leader, spoke next. He welcomed visitors and then invited two core members to stand beside him. On his right stood Greg Lannan, who has had a withered arm since the age of four. Greg was my best man. On his left was Thelus George. She had lived in a house with Judy earlier that summer, during which time she had broken her leg. Nathan gently described Daybreak as a place where those whose lives are not quite perfect, those who live with brokenness and pain, find community. We walk—we hobble—together. Our brokenness does not cut us off from one another but rather calls us into unity. It was a powerful parable.

JUDY: We are Anglicans; my sister Susan, an Anglican priest, was to have officiated and celebrated the Eucharist at our wedding. Upset as she was by what was happening, she led us all through the liturgy with much grace. During the hymns that Alan and I had chosen, we cried tears of grief, anguish, joy, and longing...longing for the unity, the love, the reality of which they spoke.... "Come down, O love divine, seek thou this soul of mine...." It was two years before I could again sing "The Servant Song":

> I will weep when you are weeping,
> when you laugh I'll laugh with you.
> I will share your joy and sorrow,
> 'til we've seen this journey through.

Henri changed the readings from those that we'd chosen for a wedding, and he preached an extempore homily on Matthew 6: "Consider the lilies of the field...your heavenly Father knows your needs.... Do not worry.... Each day has enough troubles of its own." With grace and humor he assured us all once again of God's presence, of our goodness, and that our decision was important and honest, not frivolous. He invited everyone to share prayers aloud; this gave people the chance to express their feelings and thoughts. He invited us all to feel our unity in brokenness in the Eucharist in which we were about to partake. He encouraged me and Judy to go forward with our plan to be the cupbearers around the circle; that way we could all look each other in the eye over the blood of Jesus which had been poured out for forgiveness and healing. Never has a Eucharist meant so much to us.

In the space that followed we felt lifted up to a place of peace, of quiet trust and inexplicable joy. Susan broke the silence by announcing that there was a lot of food upstairs to be eaten! After all, a banquet had been prepared. Henri said that we should all eat together as we had planned and talk to each other over the meal. Again, he saw how our fellowship could be enhanced. He was right. It was a fabulous party. Everyone had gathered that day to celebrate family, our connectedness, to demonstrate our love and support for one another, and just to *be together.* That we did. The fact that there had not been an actual legal union became less important as we all realized that we were celebrating what we had come for—being together through all of life's significant moments. We also knew that, as God's people, we can choose to respond not as the world would have us do but with vision "from above," which completely changes how we live the difficult moments of life.

We felt at peace as the day drew to a close. Our friendship was still intact, our knowledge of one another had been deepened, our love for our friends and community greatly heightened. When we tell this story, we say, "If you want to know you are loved (by your friends, your family), get married. If you want to know you are *really loved,* don't get married!" We celebrated more deeply and more meaningfully that day than we could have ever imagined. A small miracle happened, too. At the end of the Eucharist, we learned later, the clouds and heavy overcast of the day broke open, rays of

bright sunlight shone down, and, across the fields wet and glisten-
ing with raindrops, a brilliant rainbow appeared over the Dayspring.

It was not an easy time, the weeks that followed. Naturally
there was much anger, grief, confusion, and there were important
questions to work through.

JUDY: Some people have asked me, "What led you to be able
to say yes again to Alan?" It struck me as an odd question until
I realized that I had never stopped saying yes. I never said, "I
don't want to marry you." For me, the days that followed our
"non-wedding day" were very painful and sad, but also deeply
joyful and full of persevering love. It was a time of living by
faith day by day. The words of Viktor Frankl helped me: "That
which is to give light must endure burning."

Other folks were astounded that I responded the way I did,
rather than breaking off the relationship and walking away in
bitterness and anger. But at the moment Alan confessed his inner turmoil to me, I was only a few hours away from promising
to be faithful and stand by him, even in difficult times. How
deep would my commitment to that promise have been if it
could have evaporated in a mo-
ment of blazing anger and hurt?
I had been about to promise
"for better or worse." I just
didn't know we would have the
"worse" before we got the "better." But as I lived through those
difficult few weeks, I knew that
my promise, once made, would
be true.

Alan and Judy Steers
with Henri.

By the end of the month I had proposed to Judy again—she insisted, saying the first proposal had expired! We were married in October. At our wedding we recited Psalm 126:

> *The Lord has done great things for us, and we rejoice. . . .*
> *Those who go out weeping, bearing the seed for sowing,*
> *Shall come home with shouts of joy, carrying their sheaves.*

The altar was decorated with sheaves of wheat. Henri preached the homily and reminded us always, in every circumstance, to be thankful.

On a warm summer night in late August 1996, Henri, just back from his sabbatical year, stopped at our house on his way from somewhere, to somewhere, in order to visit briefly with us and especially to cuddle our newborn daughter, Emily. Three weeks later, our baby in our arms, we—with many, many others—wept, waved sunflowers, and sang "Jubilate" as we said good-bye to our dear friend. Thank you, Henri. We are grateful for your life and for the way in which you touched our lives.

Faith, Friendship, Peacemaking

ART LAFFIN

Art Laffin has been active in the faith-based nonviolent movement for peace and justice for over twenty years and is a member of the Dorothy Day Catholic Worker Community in Washington, D.C. He coedited Swords into Plowshares *and coauthored* The Risk of the Cross, *for which Henri wrote the foreword. Art and Henri became friends while Henri was teaching at Yale Divinity School.*

I first heard of Henri Nouwen in 1977, when I lived in Holland and at L'Arche in France. During that time I read his book *With Open Hands* and was deeply moved. Little did I know that Henri, a priest, renowned teacher and writer, and future member of L'Arche, and I, a lay Catholic involved in a ministry of service and peacemaking, would become good friends. Through his friendship, which spanned eighteen years, his passion to serve God and others, his dedication to the spiritual life, his heartfelt generosity, his commitment to proclaiming the Gospel of Peace, and his writing, Henri had a profound impact on my life and vocation.

I met Henri in 1978 in New Haven, Connecticut, when he was teaching at Yale Divinity School and several friends and I were forming the Covenant Peace Community (CPC). I frequently attended the Eucharist he offered at Yale, and on several occasions I sat in on his classes and joined him at his home for prayer.

Henri became a special friend of the CPC and taught and helped us in many ways. Almost weekly for over a year he would celebrate Eucharist with us. These eucharistic celebrations were at the heart of our relationship and they enabled us to grow in love for God and neighbor as we proclaimed the Gospel of Peace. They would be followed by breakfast, spiritual reading, and reflection. We discussed many things, including the role of prayer and community in a life of resistance and the importance of cultivating a spiritual life that could sustain activism. Henri warned that if we did not create a "spiritual basement" for our lives, it would be impossible for us to be sustained over the long haul. Like Thomas Merton, he was able to help me and others see the reciprocal relationship between prayer and action. Henri took great interest in our prayer life, our service to the poor, our nonviolent resistance to the arms race, and our speaking in schools and churches about Jesus' way of nonviolence. In addition to his spiritual guidance, Henri was very generous in offering financial support for our ministry.

Henri's own peacemaking journey, however, was not an easy one. Having been a chaplain in the Dutch army, he had to reconcile his military past with Jesus' call to peacemaking. In a manuscript on peacemaking, written in 1984 and posthumously published in *The Road to Peace*, Henri wrote:

> For a long time, I have sensed within me a strong hesitation to speak or write about peace. . . . Much of this hesitation goes back to my time spent in the Dutch army. . . . However, it wasn't only my Dutch army experience that made me hesitant to join the peace movement. My obser-

vations of the style, language, and behavior often exhibited at anti-war
rallies in the 1960s had made me skeptical about the value of much
anti-war activity. . . . Even today, having become deeply convinced of the
immorality of the fabrication, possession, and use of nuclear weapons, I
still feel quite nervous about speaking or acting for peace. . . . But all
these memories and emotions do not diminish the truth that the call to
peace is a call for all people regardless of their many differences.*

As a follower of Jesus, Henri came to believe, and passionately
proclaim, that saying yes to the God of Life meant saying no to all
the violence of heart and mind. In his peacemaking manuscript he
declared, "Peacemaking requires clear resistance to death in all its
manifestations."

Many people and experiences influenced Henri's thinking
about peace and justice. A major influence early on was the civil
rights movement. Henri's concern for racial equality dates back to
1965, when he participated in the historic civil rights march from
Selma to Montgomery, Alabama. Hearing Martin Luther King, Jr.,
speak, associating with civil rights workers, and attending King's
funeral all had a profound impact on him. Henri also opposed the
Vietnam War and spoke at a moratorium rally against the war at
Yale in May 1972.

A peace concern of foremost importance for Henri was the
need for worldwide nuclear disarmament. Henri believed that, in
response to the threat of global annihilation, Christians should act
out of faith, not fear; out of love, not anger. Over time he devel-

---

*Henri's spirituality of peacemaking is well-articulated in John Dear, ed., *The Road to
Peace* (Maryknoll, N.Y.: Orbis Books, 1998), a collection of Henri's talks and writings
on peace and justice that I highly recommend. This quotation comes from "Peace, a
Gift We Receive in Prayer," pp. 4–5. The two subsequent quotations come from "Celebrating Life," in the same collection.

oped a spirituality of peacemaking that focused on the relationship between prayer, resistance, and community (see "Living in the House of Love" in *The Road to Peace*). He believed each of these elements was crucial to the witness of peacemaking.

Still, Henri was reluctant when I met him to engage in public action for peace. But he always kept an open mind when we in the CPC and other friends would discuss this subject with him. Through our keeping him informed about peacemaking efforts and through his contacts with others, Henri's appreciation for acts of nonviolent resistance grew. After prayerful reflection and in response to a request from his students and other friends, Henri participated in several peacemaking actions at General Dynamics–Electric Boat Shipyard, producer of the Trident and nuclear attack submarines in Groton, Connecticut. These actions included protesting the launching of the USS *Corpus Christi* nuclear submarine in 1981. He shared our indignation that an instrument of terrible destruction was named after the Body of Christ. In 1985 he led the Good Friday Stations of the Cross. Of this experience he wrote:

> I have stayed away from most public forms of resistance and for a long time even had a deep resistance to resistance. . . . But when friends invited me to come closer and watch more attentively, I gradually came to realize that I might have been turned off as much by Jesus and his disciples as by these small groups of resisters. . . .
>
> Who could have dreamt [twenty years ago that] I would lead an ecumenical group of theology students . . . in prayerful resistance against an impending nuclear holocaust? . . .
>
> It was hard for me to know fully how I felt, but something new was happening to me that I had never experienced before. It was the

deep awareness that prayer was no longer a neutral event without danger. (pp. 50–53)

Henri continued to write and speak about the Gospel of Peace, be involved in certain public actions, and discern what next steps he should take for peace. Concerning his position on civil disobedience, he wrote:

So far I have not yet felt called to be arrested and go to jail for the sake of peace. I have always wondered if my going to jail would not alienate people from the cause of peace rather than attract them to it. But maybe I am concerned too much about influencing others and not enough about faithfulness to my own spiritual commitment. Frankly, I am not sure whether it is prudence or cowardice, conviction or practicality, faithfulness or fear that holds me back. I only know that what seemed so alien and unacceptable to me a few years ago now presents itself as at least an invitation to rethink my previous attitudes. (p. 54)

While Henri didn't feel he could risk arrest and imprisonment for acts of peacemaking, he was very supportive of people he knew who did. For example, he greatly supported Dean Hammer of CPC, myself, and others who were imprisoned for Plowshares actions—a nonviolent witness to disarm weapons components inspired by the biblical prophecy that swords would be beaten into plowshares. Henri's support included speaking at several Plowshares benefits, writing letters, sending books, praying for peace prisoners during the Eucharist, and, once, visiting Dean in prison and giving a retreat for him and his fellow inmates.

After he left New Haven, Henri spent time living in Guatemala, Bolivia, and Peru. He now saw that part of his ministry was to help

Peace march. Henri (center, behind crossbearer) leading 1985 Good Friday Stations of the Cross, Art Laffin at right.

people in the United States understand that their spiritual destiny was linked to that of Latin America. Following a visit to Nicaragua as part of a Witness for Peace delegation in 1983, Henri spoke across the United States about how the crucifixion of Christ was being reenacted in the oppression of the poor of Latin America. He decried U.S. intervention in Nicaragua as "unjust, illegal, and immoral." When he went to live at L'Arche Daybreak in 1986, Henri began bringing members of the community with him to his speaking engagements. He was thereby able to give voice to the voiceless, an essential part of peacemaking. Ultimately, Henri believed that actions done in faith will bear good fruit. What is most important, he believed, is that our actions spring from a place of prayer and love for God. If our actions come from a "hostile heart," he wrote, they will do more harm than good.

After Henri left Yale Divinity School we kept in contact. I continued to live in New Haven after the CPC disbanded in 1983. I was part of the Isaiah Peace Ministry until 1989. Following my imprisonment for a Plowshares action, I moved in 1990 to Washington, D.C., to be part of the Catholic Worker Community. During these years Henri was a faithful friend, always genuinely concerned about how I was and how he could support me. When I was in prison he wrote me and sent his latest book. He was an important spiritual guide, always helping me remember to stay spiritually sustained.

Henri offered me his heartfelt support following the suicide of my younger sister, Mary, in November 1988. In a beautiful letter of consolation, he wrote:

> *God certainly is asking much of you, and I can imagine how deeply wounded your heart must be by Mary's tragic death. You must feel so powerless and so deeply in anguish. . . . I want to assure you that I feel very close to you, and that my heart connects deeply with you in this experience of powerlessness. We are both called to rely completely on God's mercy for ourselves and for those with whom we are deeply connected.*

Henri's words not only conveyed a deep love for me but also reflected the anguish that he had been experiencing. Despite his own pain he was able to offer me consolation. Somehow, Henri was always able to see his pain, and the pain of others, in the context of his abiding faith in God.

I am especially grateful to Henri for giving me a renewed appreciation of the Eucharist, which has helped me immensely. The Eucharist has been and continues to be a primary sustaining force in my faith journey and ministry, which has included living in community, serving the poor and homeless, engaging in nonviolent actions to protect life, and standing with victims calling for peace in war zones in Northern Ireland, Central America, Palestine, Israel, and Iraq. The Eucharist has also helped me to endure being assaulted, being imprisoned, responding to social injustice and extreme violence, and coping with the sickness and death of family members and friends.

I can testify that the Eucharist was the center of Henri's life. Henri often reminded us that the word *Eucharist* literally means "act of thanksgiving." He believed that to live a eucharistic life means to be filled with gratitude. I always felt God's Spirit present in a powerful way when Henri broke open the Scriptures and celebrated the Eucharist. He had a great gift of helping people see that God's love is unconditional, and that without God we can do nothing.

When we celebrate the Eucharist, Henri believed our hearts should burn within us, for we are entering into divine communion. In the face of all the bad news, we proclaim in the Eucharist the Good News of salvation: Through his cross and resurrection, Jesus has forever overcome the forces of sin and death. He has ushered in God's reign of love, justice, and peace, and has shown us a new way to live. In the Eucharist, Jesus commands that we love unconditionally, and that we see each person as a sister or brother, a member of his body. Eucharistic love means renouncing all violence and killing and upholding all life as sacred, for we are all part of God.

Henri gave his life out of love for Jesus and for others. His ministry at L'Arche was a deep expression of the Eucharist. He said to those afflicted with mental and physical disabilities: "This is my body given for you." In the midst of his own struggles, Henri's life at Daybreak and especially his relationship with Adam Arnett, a severely mentally and physically handicapped man whom he befriended and cared for, was a truly liberating experience for him. To all who have eyes of faith to see, Henri showed the healing, transforming power of the Eucharist and the fruit that can be borne by living a eucharistic life.

· · ·

In early August 1996, I spoke with Henri by phone. Even though he was on sabbatical he shared how exhausted he was. I encouraged him to take care of himself. I told him he was especially remembered in my prayers and thanked him for his special friendship. He offered to make a donation to support my upcoming trip to Israel to help free Mordechai Vanunu, the imprisoned nuclear whistle-blower. Little did I know that this would be the last time I would speak with him, for God would call him home the next month.

In *The Inner Voice of Love,* Henri wrote that those you have loved deeply who have died live on in you, not just as memories but as real presences. Since his death I have felt his presence in powerful ways. Henri continues to minister to me and countless others. His life of faithfulness was a gift beyond measure—his spirit lives on!

Rediscovering

My Priesthood

WENDY LYWOOD

Wendy Lywood is an Anglican (Episcopal) priest who came to L'Arche Day-break in 1992. She continues to live in a Daybreak home, is a member of the community's pastoral team, and helps with spiritual formation at an Anglican theological college. Henri deeply influenced her ministry.

Henri Nouwen gave me an incredible gift, one that many people long to receive and so many are never offered—the gift of having a mentor. Henri was for me a role model, a teacher, a pastor, a priest, and a companion on the human journey. I do not mean to imply that Henri and I spent a lot of time together or were even close friends, but because we were members of the same community our lives were linked in a way that had a profound influence upon me, particularly my understanding of my own call to priesthood. I offer this reflection on that time we shared in gratitude for Henri, for the L'Arche Daybreak community that gave us a home, and for the mysterious love of God that invites us, as Henri often said, to discover home on the way Home.

I had been responsible for a three-point parish in rural Manitoba for three and a half years when I felt like I could not go on.

In many ways I loved parish ministry: I loved the people, I loved being in the country, I loved the privilege of accompanying parishioners through major life events, I loved leading Bible studies, and, much to my surprise, I loved preaching. Despite this, there was a deep longing in me that was not being satisfied. I longed to have people with whom I could pray and share, but that didn't seem possible where I was. I was coming to understand that my vision of Christian community and the reality of parish life didn't match.

For example, I really believed the church has an important ministry in being with people in the experience of dying and death, but I was frustrated by my inability to break through the cultural taboos about death. I was longing to find a genuine Christian response to the reality of death, but I knew that unless I could talk honestly about death I couldn't talk about the resurrection in an authentic way. It felt like there was an increasing gap between what I had hoped for and what I actually experienced. I finally realized that I had nothing left to give. I knew I needed to leave the parish and find a place where I could experience my vision of Christian community in daily life. That's how I ended up at L'Arche Daybreak in November 1992. I came burnt out, incredibly insecure, and wondering if I had misunderstood God's call in my life. I was certain that I didn't want to exercise my priesthood, that I just wanted to experience the daily life of the community.

Some of the most powerful experiences of my early time at Daybreak were in the daily Eucharist services. I was deeply nourished by the simplicity and intimacy of the gatherings. Henri encouraged people in the community to give reflections, and I felt as if I was hearing the Gospels for the first time—the direct and honest way people related to the Scriptures was like drops of water seeping into the cracked earth of my soul. I couldn't get enough of it! And I had never heard anyone preach with Henri's passion, wisdom, and simplicity. But hearing such reflections only deepened my sense of inadequacy and insecurity—I didn't want to offer reflections because I was terrified that people would witness the emptiness inside me.

Henri, however, did not let me get away with this for too long! During my first Holy Week in the community he asked if I would give the reflection on Maundy (Holy) Thursday. Even though he knew that I was struggling with my call to priesthood, he insisted on the importance of celebrating my priesthood as well as his. I now realize that this was the first of many times Henri invited me to claim more deeply my call to priesthood. He and others drew out the gift of my priesthood that I wasn't sure was there.

In November 1993, I was asked to lead a gathering of women preparing for ordination in the Church of England. I felt completely inadequate to such a task, but Henri was excited for me and a source of great encouragement. He reminded me that my habit of comparing my ministry with those of others was dangerous. He called comparison "the death of spiritual life." He spent time with me as I thought through what I would do, and he said to me, "Wendy, remember the ministry is about being present with people as you are, not as you are not. You won't say anything new or original, just speak from your heart and from your own relationship with Jesus. You're not there to solve problems but to announce that Jesus wants to love, heal, forgive, and reconcile."

About that same time, Connie Ellis, Henri's secretary, was dying of a brain tumor. Henri was in Europe writing, so I had been visiting Connie in the hospital. She took a turn for the worse, and Henri decided to come home to be with her. When he arrived he phoned to ask me to see Connie with him. I knew what a close relationship Henri and Connie had, and I had a sense that she had been waiting for him. I told Henri that I understood if he wanted to see Connie on his own, but he insisted that because I had been the one visiting Connie, he would like to go with me. I'm so glad he insisted because I will never forget that encounter.

I waited near the back of the room as Henri and Connie greeted one another. The image I have is of Henri's large frame bent over and enveloping Connie, as if he were a bird protecting its young. He took her hand tenderly in his; then he asked me if I would read the Gospel for the day. It was from Luke 4, where Jesus reads from the scroll of the prophet Isaiah. Henri then spoke with gentle authority: "Connie, this reading has a special meaning for you. You are poor as you face your death, but Jesus wants you to know that he has good news for you: that he will not abandon you even as you journey through death. You are captive now in your body, but you will be released. You are blind now, because you can't see what lies ahead, but you will soon see anew in the kingdom of God. You are oppressed now, but soon you will be free." I was shocked at first by Henri's directness, but there was also a great longing awakened within me; a truth was being spoken that I needed to hear.

Henri taught me and our community a lot about how to be-friend death. We walked through it with Maurice, Connie, Hank, Lloyd, Helen, and Adam. Each time we learned to trust more that when we could share our deepest sorrows, we would touch in the same place our deepest joys. Henri helped us articulate that joy and sorrow are two sides of the same coin.

I remember that after Lloyd Kerman died we gathered in the chapel. Henri was sitting at the front and asking people to share what Lloyd's death meant to them. Michael Arnett, one of Lloyd's good friends, cried out, "My heart is broken! What does it mean, my heart is broken?" Michael's question pierced through our grief. Henri leapt out of his chair and ran to kneel in front of Michael.

"It means you have a heart that loves and that you especially loved Lloyd, Michael. Now that Lloyd has died, your heart has a big hole in it; that is why it hurts so much." I was moved not only by Michael's honesty and ability to articulate his pain but also by Henri's response. It was not so much what he said but the way his whole being became compassion. It seemed to me that both Michael and Henri were profoundly incarnational—Michael's pain and Henri's compassion were both experienced in the fullness of their humanity. In the Gospels when we are told that Jesus had compassion for the people, the Greek word used means that he was moved in his guts. Henri was following in the footsteps of Jesus in being such a compassionate pastor—he didn't hold back in fear, he didn't need to keep a professional distance.

Likewise, Henri had a passion about wakes. He and other leaders in the community knew that for the core members to grieve well they needed to participate in concrete ways in the mourning process. Henri encouraged people to come to the open casket, to touch the body, to leave a drawing or memento, and to pray. I remember at one wake he invited everyone to make a big circle around the casket. I had no idea what he was up to, but it proved to be another of those moments that opened something for me. Henri greeted us all and invited us to listen to Scripture. He then asked a few people who had been close to the person who died to share stories about their relationship.

The deep quality of the sharing had a lot to do with the core members' ability to express their feelings, but Henri's ministry allowed their natural gifts to blossom and bless everyone there. This was a far cry from the hushed tones and awkwardness of my previous visits to a funeral home. The result was a deeply healing experience of community as we cried our sorrows and laughed our love. It was so hopeful. I began to discover that it is the journey into the reality of death that allows us to find hope springing from our shared grief. It sounds obvious, but the only way to get to the hope offered in the resurrection is to go through death, not around it.

My call to priesthood and the grief of facing death came together when we were preparing for Henri's funeral. I knew that it would be a Roman Catholic Eucharist and, therefore, if I vested as an Anglican priest I would not be able to receive communion. This was a formal occasion, and, strictly speaking, those who are not Roman Catholic cannot receive communion in a Catholic mass. But Henri's support of my priesthood was so important that I decided I would wear my robes. It was, therefore, very painful for me not to be able to receive the nourishment of the Eucharist. I asked the presiding priest if he would give a blessing to some Anglican clergy who had not received communion, and he invited me to do that with him. On my way back to my seat I passed by a line of people who had just received communion. A woman I did not know took my hand, shook it, and said, "This is a gift from Henri to you." She had given me half of her communion wafer. It was such a moment of grace and inclusive love!

Henri gave me a copy of *Can You Drink the Cup?* in September 1996, just before he died. In it he had written:

> *Peace, joy, hope, courage, confidence, and lots of trust,*
> *Henri*

Henri's mentoring of me helped me open up my life to receive these gifts. Thanks be to God!

ON GRATITUDE

The discipline of gratitude is the explicit effort to acknowledge that all I am and have is given to me as a gift of love, a gift to be celebrated with joy.

There is always the choice between resentment and gratitude because God has appeared in my darkness, urged me to come home, and declared in a voice filled with affection: "You are with me always, and all I have is yours." Indeed, I can choose . . . to lament about the many misfortunes which have plagued me in the past, and thereby wrap myself up in my resentment. But I don't have to do this. There is the option to look into the eyes of the One who came out to search for me and see therein that all I am and all I have is pure gift calling for gratitude.

The choice for gratitude rarely comes without some real effort. But each time I make it, the next choice is a little easier, a little freer, a little less self-conscious. Because every gift I acknowledge reveals another and another, until finally even the most normal, obvious, and seemingly mundane event or encounter proves to be filled with grace.

—*The Return of the Prodigal Son*

My Trips
with Henri

THELUS GEORGE

*Thelus George came to L'Arche Daybreak in 1972. She is a member of the
Daybreak Seniors' Club and is known for her fine baking. Thelus enjoyed
traveling with Henri. On her first trip with him, Henri received an honorary
degree. On her second he spoke to the General Convention of the Episcopal
Church. Thelus asked Kathy Kelly and Wendy Lywood to help her prepare
this contribution.*

Henri was a nice guy. I went on trips with him.

Henri asked me, Come to Indiana. Earlham College. Kim came
too. We stayed with Henri's friend—a nice lady. I had my own
room. Henri said sit on the stage with him. He talked to the people. He had his eyes closed, waving his hands around, close to the
edge. I was afraid he'd fall off the stage!

Another trip, I went to Indianapolis. At the airport there was a
big car for us—white, a stretch limousine. It had a telephone.
Henri dialed and I phoned the Seniors at Daybreak from the car.

Henri asked me and Wendy to be in a skit. I was sad and
Wendy was Jesus and she come over and touched my head. Then
he talked to the priests. We stayed in a nice hotel. I met David from

Thelus George and Henri.

New York. After that, David came to visit Daybreak. He likes my carrot cake.

When I joined my church, Henri came. Henri said I'm a nice lady. He came to my church for Lloyd's funeral too. He talked about Lloyd. Lloyd was in the Seniors' Club.

He came to my birthday, prayed for me.

Henri said, "Jesus with you."

Henri Nouwen
as Mystic

GEORGE STROHMEYER

George Strohmeyer is a Roman Catholic diocesan priest who cofounded the L'Arche community in Erie, Pennsylvania, in 1972. He continues to live in the community and is a chaplain at Gannon University. George knew Henri as a friend and brother priest in L'Arche and was the celebrant for Henri's funeral mass in Markham, Ontario.

Henri Nouwen was a strong presence for me in the ten years that he lived in L'Arche. He had a mystical consciousness of oneness. In our rational, egoic thinking about him, we could say that perhaps he should have been more theologically rigorous, more politically visible in the post–Vatican II church in Holland, or have taken more public stands on more issues in and out of the church in America; we could even say that he should have been less vain or not so concerned about the admiration of others; and that he should have been more physically settled during silent prayer and more quiet at 4:30 in the morning. And, as a mystic, he should have looked and acted more like one. He should have written fewer books, spent more time in silence, and experienced more inner peace and tranquility. But Henri did not fit stereotypes. I want to make two observations about Henri as a contemplative mystic.

First, Henri's mystical heart and mystical journey were not often manifested in his writing of books directly on the subject nor in his formal teaching of methods of contemplative prayer. This is not to minimize the excellence of his book *The Way of the Heart,* which helped develop my own appreciation of contemplative prayer and which I have used in teaching many L'Arche assistants. Where Henri's mystical path *was* evident was in the continual purification and transformation of his psyche—a transformation that he experienced and revealed in the many relationships and pastoral demands of day-to-day life. He journeyed gradually into deep awareness, transcendence, and freedom. His path led him to the profound discovery that everything about him, from the humiliating to the exalting, was just as God foresaw, just as God blessed him to be. Henri became the personification of the Zen maxim "All things are as it is."

Second, because he was a mystic contemplative, Henri's marketplace, his context for living out his life, was literally the world. He was full of joyful determination, throwing himself unreservedly into life's experiences, extraordinarily generous with his time, his energy, his money. He came to realize his hidden identity: before all else he knew he was beloved of God. And he knew the secret identity of each of us. His motivation—his deep desire to realize his own hidden potential and to awaken the hidden potential in others—carried him beyond himself and his physical capacities. When he ministered, Henri was full of seemingly unhindered, life-giving energy. He radiated the essence of God taking form in his body, mind, and spirit.

The Benedictine sister Jean Lavin, one of my Zen associates, remarked of the energy coming from Henri's mystical depth, "It takes intuition to look into the face of Henri and see behind his eyes and hear beyond his words the direct experience of the essence of spiritual things about which he wanted so deeply to speak and write in a spiritual way. Henri possessed, radiated, and lived mystical consciousness and it was his fundamental identity."

The ten famous ox-herding pictures of the old Zen masters describe the universal stages of spiritual cultivation. It would be possible to follow the development of Henri's spiritual path and ministry through all ten pictures or stages, but I will settle for the last stage: The seeker, having searched for the ox (the symbol of one's true nature), having found the ox, arrives at the high point of his journey by coming back to the marketplace without the ox. Here is the text as recorded by Wong Kiew Kit in his *Complete Book of Zen:*

> *Entering the marketplace with bare chest and feet,*
> *Covered with mud and dust but smiling broadly,*
> *There's no need for the magic of saints and gods;*
> *Even dried trees he can make to flower sweetly.* *

I paraphrase the author as he continues: The seeker returns to the everyday world to help those in need regardless of race, culture, religion. His chest is bare; he has nothing to hide. In his bare feet he is ready to go to the lowest levels to help. He does not sneer at the vanity and futility of mundane life but smiles broadly. The seeker has miraculous power, which he always uses for the good of others. The secret to this power is a mind focused and concen-

---

* Rockport, Mass.: Element Books, 1998.

trated. He makes no attempt to follow earlier sages as he goes on his way.

If we do not see the mystical qualities in Henri, we are left with a caricature: his words as they reflect only his rational intelligence or his uncanny talent to reveal himself so openly. If we do not permit Henri's transformed self to invite us to greater awareness, the loss might in the end be that we would not grasp the invitation that Henri was and is still as an instrument to help us come to know and cherish our own true nature, the very identity of the Absolute Reality in me as me, in you as you, in each of us as us.

After Henri met Anton Boisen, founder of the clinical pastoral counseling movement, he wrote of how Boisen's "deep wound [had] become a source of beauty in which even the weaknesses seem to give light" and of how the wound could thus be "a reason for thankfulness."* Henri was writing this of himself as well as of Boisen and, I will add, of all of us. But he is not asking us to simply be grateful or to relax and accept our brokenness. Henri the mystic takes his place next to us in the painful and intoxicating reality of being fully human, fully alive, fully himself, because his life, his meaning, his purpose is nothing less than this. And Henri invites us to do nothing less.

Henri comes to the end of his journey to nothingness and is thus exalted. He finishes the task given to him and becomes a transparent icon, a window through which we can see who we are and why we are. We come forth and we return to the oneness of Absolute Reality, or, if you like, love—wholeness—shalom—God.

---

* Quoted in Michael Ford, *Wounded Prophet* (Doubleday, 1999).

Making Dreams Come True

FRED BRATMAN

Fred Bratman is a marketing executive at an investment bank in New York. He is also the author of several books for young adults. He and Henri became friends while Henri was teaching at Yale. Henri wrote the book Life of the Beloved *in response to a suggestion from Fred.*

Some debts can never be repaid. And some aren't meant to be. My friendship with Henri Nouwen celebrated the inherent joy of life despite its inevitable hardships.

I met Henri in about 1980 when I wrote a brief profile of him for a newspaper. He was teaching at Yale and I was just out of graduate school, trying to figure out how to cobble together two coherent sentences. When we met I didn't want to let on how green and unseasoned I was, but I am sure Henri saw right through me. The day we spent together in New Haven, Henri asked me more questions than I got to ask him. Every time I answered his question he had another one for me. He could see that I was struggling to find my place in the world and make writing my vocation.

Our backgrounds could not have been more different. I was twenty-three, Jewish, and cynical. He was forty-four, a Catholic priest, and a recognized writer. I did get enough information from him to write my piece, and I thought that would be the end of it. But Henri had different ideas. A few days later he called me and asked if we could meet when he visited New York the following week. I lived in a studio apartment—a euphemism for a closet—in Manhattan. Its one benefit was a door that opened onto the building's roof. He came on a sunny, warm spring day and we drank cold beer while watching the traffic below whiz by. To this day I can't understand why he made his generous offer, but my lack of understanding hasn't diminished my appreciation. He invited me to come to Yale for a year and write. Now, what was this guy's angle? He was a virtual stranger offering me the chance of a lifetime. But he hadn't read a word I wrote, so encouraging a great undiscovered talent could not have been his rationale. No, instead he nurtured a dream—my dream.

That year in New Haven was when our friendship took root. During that year and for years later I often found myself part of Henri's life in ways I couldn't have imagined. I visited the dying and the emotionally troubled with him and watched him minister. I visited him in a Trappist monastery and baked bread with monks, going out of my way to see if I could make them laugh. I dined in elegant homes on Fifth Avenue, where white-gloved waiters served lunch on fine china. And I drove with him to Hamilton, Ontario, to watch him talk at the Catholic Worker Community and serve food to the homeless.

I soon saw that what Henri had done for me he had also done for scores of others—and always with no strings attached. He gave with few expectations. He was far from reckless but was committed to making a difference in the lives of the people who crossed his path. His primary expectation was that you keep your heart open to life. In my case his support led me to give up my cloak of cynicism. He helped me see that the hardships and setbacks that are part of life don't diminish its beauty or wonder. If anything they provide the necessary contrast.

Henri embraced the love that is innate in life and refused to accept the notion that life is petty, brutish, or random. Several years after my time at Yale, I watched him give a lecture to a packed auditorium. At the center of a blackboard he wrote the date of his birth—1932—and then drew a short line across to a point which he marked 2010, with a question mark next to it. He turned and said, "This could represent my life, a finite period with a beginning and an end." He paused for a moment and gently shook his head. He went back to the blackboard and drew a line from one end all the way across to the other end. He said, "I have come from somewhere and I am going someplace else." He saw himself as a player in an unfolding masterpiece, and he was grateful for his part.

About a year before he died Henri visited me for the last time. He insisted on buying my three-year-old son a present. A truck, ball, or book wouldn't do. He demanded that the gift be special, special enough so that Jacob would remember him. Jacob wanted in-line skates. Most people would have thought him far too young for a present that demanded such dexterity. But the impracticality of the gift only inspired Henri. We bought them, and when we buckled them on Jacob's feet, Henri's smile could not have been wider. He had made another dream come true.

The Necessity
of Prayer

LORENZO
SFORZA-CESARINI

Lorenzo Sforza-Cesarini was born in Rome. He traveled widely and stud-
ied in California before coming to L'Arche Daybreak in 1986. He works in
the Woodery and serves on the Daybreak pastoral team, which Henri invited
him to join at its inception. Henri was Lorenzo's spiritual director. This con-
tribution is based on a tape-recorded conversation with Philip Coulter.

The spiritual journey that led me to L'Arche and Henri began in
my own family. The Sforzas were a powerful northern Italian family who became dukes of Milan. As a child I had a life filled with
privilege. We had a palazzo with a courtyard, and my grandmother
and grandfather had their own chauffeur. I'd go to parties thrown
by people from the same social milieu as we were. Servants would
treat me, a small boy, with great deference. Even then I saw the
contrast between my world and the real world of ordinary people
with ordinary jobs. Even then I felt that there was some kind of injustice about all this.

I think the sense of social justice that I have today sprang out
of my own suffering. I was born with a cleft palate, and I've got hip

dysplasia. So early on I discovered that the world isn't very fair. I guess my bitter suffering made me more sensitive to other people's suffering. And I guess somewhere in the chambers of my heart, faith was alive. As a child I would go to church, and I would pray, and frequently I was quite desperate. The one thing I asked for in my prayers was that God would give me good people to be with when I grew up.

As I grew up I became friends with a priest who lived next door to us. His name was Pierre Riches, and he took an interest in my spiritual development. He was good friends with the Vaniers, Pauline and Georges, so he knew about Jean and about L'Arche. One day when we were on a train he told me about the L'Arche community at Trosly-Breuil in France. So I went there for a visit. Trosly seemed like a lunar landscape, a totally different world for me, but that short visit eventually led me to Daybreak.

Some years later I asked Pierre Riches, "Why did you encourage me to go to Trosly?"

"Well, you were unhappy," he said, "you were unhappy."

When I first came to Daybreak in 1986, I lived in a house that had many people with disabilities. Very often there were difficult situations; nevertheless I decided to stick with it.

Soon after I arrived Henri came to be the pastor for the community. The first time I met him was at a training session for assistants, and my first impression was that he was very particular. I can't think of any other word to describe it. He had something in his face that was out of the ordinary: a sparkle in his expression and in his eyes. And he was so alive! He obviously had something in him that I could really benefit from. Here, I felt, was someone who could take the place of Pierre Riches for me. So I decided to ask Henri if he would be my spiritual director. "I would like to do that"—that's all he said. The fact that he was also a psychologist

and that he had an enormous faith, an enormous desire to follow
God in his own life, in his own journey, was important to me.

We would meet for spiritual direction in a little chapel at Daybreak. We would be seated on straight-backed chairs in the middle
of the room, facing each other knee to knee. Henri would be very
attentive. He asked about my family, about me, about what had
happened to me, really drilling me with questions about my life. I
felt that here was someone who was interested in me, who wanted
to discover what there was in me. Henri really wanted to know
what my spiritual journey was about, what my turning points were,
what was going on inside me.

He would ask me about prayer and about my faith. Then he
would explain what, in his opinion, was going on in me, what had
happened. He could be very much the psychologist, very analyti-
cal. Then he would add the spiritual aspect of what he felt was going on in me. My biggest craving—then and now—was for
affection. I was filled with desire to be loved. Henri would get into
the history of that, go back and analyze where all this need might
have come from. And then he would tell me that God accepts me
for who I am.

Henri was a very tender man who had a lot of caring for other
people. We had a good friendship even though his life was so busy
that I often felt disconnected from him. Sometimes I would see
him only twice a year, and although he was very present to me
when we met, I felt a longing to have more time with him and a
sadness that I would never be really, really close to him.

Henri was the kind of friend who really believed in you. And
as a result I really believed in him, too. I discovered that we had
similar struggles with the affective side of our lives. He told me
that he too longed for intimacy in friendships and sometimes felt
that he didn't have any intimacy at all; sometimes he felt quite

lonely, quite abandoned. So I came to realize that he understood my feelings very deeply. Many times he'd say, "You know, you and I have the same problem."

I don't think he had an answer for his struggle, and he didn't have an answer for me either. But prayer was always the big suggestion. "Bring it to God," he would say. To him, prayer meant total surrender. Total surrender of his issues and his struggles, a total offering up of everything he held most deep in himself to God. I think that was why, when he talked about prayer in public, he was extremely animated, because he wanted people to get that message.

I believe that Henri understood prayer in a way few people do; it's such a mystery for all of us, but it wasn't so much of a mystery for Henri. In his heart Henri knew that prayer was an answer to the many, many struggles he had. Prayer gave him the freedom from his deepest longings that he so much wanted, and this was true for me, too. So he encouraged me greatly to use prayer. And I have to say that I really struggled against this. Then one day I decided to follow his advice and just do it. So now every night I pray.

Another thing Henri would do as my spiritual director was bring me books—all kinds of books, including books he wrote—that he thought might be helpful for me. He gave me a Bible, which today I use with great reverence, as well as an abbreviated version of the breviary. That was something he used very eloquently. And I still have the little handwritten note he gave me suggesting how I should use it.

But the process Henri guided me through had prayer at its center. I realize that now. The thing prayer has taught me is that I'm loved. Even though sometimes it's hard for me to believe that, I've found that there is a place where it's really, really safe and welcoming, and I can really be my broken self. There is a safe place, and that's in prayer. I can't bring all of my brokenness to any one place in this physical world, but I can bring it to prayer. And I can let go and still know that I'm loved. And that, I think, is the essence of what Henri tried to teach me.

One last thought: My family name, Sforza, was the nickname for an ancient ancestor, a tribute to his zest for life. If you take away the *S* in *Sforza,* you're left with *forza,* which is the Italian word for strength. But if you put the *S* in front, then it's the word for making an effort. And maybe that's the best I can say for myself—I'm making an effort. And for that I thank Henri.

Hands of Love

JOE VORSTERMANS

Joe Vorstermans is the lay pastor of L'Arche Daybreak, a role Henri encouraged him to accept shortly before Henri died. Joe is studying for his master of divinity degree. He and his wife, Stephanie, have been at Daybreak for more than twenty years. They have four children.

Every time I see a dead person I am unprepared for the stillness. It happened again at Henri's wake.

The Daybreak community was gathered together in our meeting hall, praying and singing, while we waited for Henri's body to arrive from the airport. It had been nearly a week since Henri died, and those days had been full as we prepared for his wake and funeral. We had designated this evening as a time for the community and close friends to be together with Henri's body. We wanted a quiet time to grieve, pray, and comfort each other.

I went to meet those who had arrived with Henri's body and helped them bring the casket into the foyer. Joe Child removed the casket's lid and lifted Henri's head slightly so he could place a pillow underneath. Henri's face was grayish and slack. His mouth looked unnatural, stiff. He was dressed in a white alb and one of the woolen stoles that he so often wore while celebrating the Eucharist in the Dayspring chapel. I was feeling lost as I tried to see the man we knew in this body. The features were familiar, but the stillness was foreign. His hands saddened me even more. They too were grayish. The skin was transparent and drawn so that the bones protruded. His fingers were intertwined with a rosary that dug into the skin. His hands were folded on his chest. They were cold and still.

All week I had felt guided by Henri's spirit as we alternated between grieving for him and working to plan his funeral. He had been so present. Now I was overwhelmed by the emptiness expressed in his face and hands. These lips that had spoken words of hope and love, that had encouraged us so often to wait in expectation for the goodness hidden in the pain, were now lifeless. These lips that had spoken the prayers of mercy, blessing, and consecration so often in our little chapel were lifeless. These lips that had cried in anguish when we couldn't fulfill his expectations were slack. It seemed so wrong that they were not moving. And these hands that had blessed us, that had gripped our shoulders and stroked our backs, how could they be so still?

The people inside were waiting, and we carried Henri in and placed him in front, surrounded by his friends. I stood before the community with no idea of what to say or how to begin. Henri's brother Laurent came in with Sue Mosteller and Nathan Ball. They had flown from Holland with Henri's body. They looked shaken and exhausted.

I reminded people about the many times Henri had come to and gone from Daybreak to fulfill his mission to announce the Word and to be with family and friends. Always we sent him off and welcomed him home again. Tonight we were gathered to welcome him home and send him off one last time.

We told stories about him. "I remember," someone would say, and they'd tell about a moment shared with Henri that would be humorous or enlightening. We would all laugh or nod in understanding, and one memory would spark another.

After the stories I invited each person to come forward and touch Henri, to say a prayer with him, or to place something in his casket. I stood at the foot of the casket and witnessed how each person lived that moment with Henri. It was beautiful to watch. I realized more fully how Henri had managed to meet each person at the place of his or her pain and gift. Now each person stood with him in grief and with gratitude. So many of those who came forward laid their hands over his and rested them there as if wanting to recapture the many blessings they had received from him in the years gone by. Some placed a flower, a photo, a handmade card or picture in the casket.

Doug McCarthy, a Jesuit priest, came forward. He stood still and straight as one priest before another. He touched Henri's hand, turned away, and came toward me. He placed both his hands on my shoulders and said a blessing on me: "Joe, you are called to be the pastor of Daybreak. I will support you." At first the words offended me. It seemed an inappropriate time to think about anything but our loss. I had no desire to be the pastor. I only wished that Henri had not died. However, Doug's words were in fact a restatement of a call I had received from Henri a few months earlier.

When the wake was over and everyone had gone home, I took my moment with Henri and remembered. I recalled the way he had befriended me at a time of great pain, when my marriage to Stephanie was fragile and I was feeling hopeless. Henri had a remarkable capacity to trust that pain would be redeemed by new life. He also saw gifts in me that I could not recognize and invited me to work with him in pastoral situations. Only the week before

Henri left on his last trip, the Daybreak community had affirmed me to take on the role of lay pastor so that when Henri returned he would have more time to write while continuing to fulfill his priestly role of bringing the sacraments. I had so looked forward to learning from and working closely with Henri. I felt broken-hearted as my deep disappointment welled up from within. I looked at Henri's hands again.

I placed my hands over them and remembered how these hands had broken the bread during the daily Eucharist. Henri always broke the bread so completely and with such careful deliberation. The tragedy of pain was made evident in the breaking. The suffering of each person was revealed. His suffering was always evident too, the torment that he experienced because he was so gifted and yet so vulnerable to his need to be accepted.

All of this fragility was surrounded by his hands. Those hands that were so large, expressive, and gentle. His hands held the broken body of Jesus, within which were the broken bodies of the members of Daybreak. Amidst all the fragility, Henri stood, for us and with us. He stood with the impossible assurance that broken-ness is not the last word. That brokenness, if held, will be redeemed into new life. At these moments I experienced that my own humanness was truly carved in the palm of God's hand and held there.

I remembered how Henri's hands surrounded the clear glass chalice that revealed the blood of Christ to all who were gathered. How deliberately he raised the cup and offered it up for us and with us. How much Henri desired to raise us up from the difficulties of life so we could be touched by the warmth of God's love. I remembered the way his hands held the chalice so firmly, yet surrounded it with tenderness. When I watched Henri raise the cup high at the consecration, I would feel held and raised up to be embraced by God.

Those hands of the Eucharist were equally firm and tender when he placed them on our shoulders to comfort or encourage us. For a brief moment he would hold us and invite us to be aware and accepting of our vulnerabilities. He seemed to stand still in empathy and recognition before he would squeeze a little harder to say, It's time to move beyond our pain and go forth to serve others.

Those personal moments were consecrations of our humanity. Henri held our broken bodies, blessed us, and sent us forth to be fruitful.

How often in the years since his death I have wished to feel Henri's hands on my shoulders, like the prodigal son in the Rembrandt painting. Those hands of understanding and empathy. Those hands of love.

LOVE DEEPLY

Do not hesitate to love and to love deeply. You might be afraid of the pain that love can cause. When those you love deeply reject you, leave you, or die, your heart will be broken. But that should not hold you back from loving deeply. The pain that comes from deep love makes your love ever more fruitful. It is like a plow that breaks the ground to allow the seed to take root and grow into a strong plant. Every time you experience the pain of rejection, absence, or death, you are faced with a choice. You can become bitter and decide not to love again, or you can stand straight in your pain and let the soil on which you stand become richer and more able to give life to new seeds.

The more you have loved and have allowed yourself to suffer because of your love, the more you will be able to let your heart grow wider and deeper. When your love is truly giving and receiving, those whom you love will not leave your heart even when they depart from you. They will become part of your self and thus gradually build a community within you.

The wider your inner community becomes, the more easily you will recognize your own brothers and sisters in the strangers you see around you. As you love deeply, the ground of your heart will be broken more and more, but you will rejoice in the abundance of the fruit it will bear.

—*The Inner Voice of Love*

A Gentle
Instrument of
a Loving God

JEAN VANIER

Jean Vanier is an inspirational speaker, writer, and leader in the lay faith com-
munity movement. He is known for his prophetic voice calling for the recog-
nition of those who are most marginal in society and is a spiritual mentor for
people of all ages, cultures, and religions. He lives with people who have dis-
abilities in the original L'Arche community, which he founded in Trosly-
Breuil, France, in 1964.

I first met Henri Nouwen in 1981 at a retreat for people from our
different communities who had come together to deepen their
commitment to L'Arche. He had mentioned L'Arche in his book
Clowning in Rome, and I felt he understood what we were trying to
do and that it would be good for us to meet. So it was that we had
time to share together, and our friendship began.

Our friendship deepened when, a few years later, he came to
live for a while in Trosly, the French community where L'Arche
started. At the time he seemed dissatisfied with his career as a

Henri and Jean Vanier.

teacher at Harvard University and appeared to be in search of something else, perhaps a "home" where he could put down roots.

And I think Henri found a kind of home here. He spent a year with us, living in a house that belonged to my mother and sharing meals with the community. He made many friends; he was delighted to spend time with my mother, and he particularly loved to share with Father Thomas Philippe, the Dominican priest with whom I had begun L'Arche. He also loved to spend time with the assistants, those who are called to share their lives with the men and women in the community who have disabilities.

I think Henri felt a bit frustrated with me, however. He considered friendship deeply important, and to him that meant we should always be on call for each other. My life, though, was rooted in my community. I spent my time with those who had disabilities, in my household, or in meetings, or accompanying assistants. I was able to meet with Henri only now and again for an hour or so, and this hurt him. I could understand that. But my days were full. He, by contrast, had time on his hands, felt quite lonely, was searching for a home. So we lived our lives in different ways. All of this meant that our friendship became a bit strained. But I don't think that either of us forgot the fact that between us there was a deep mutual love; we were brothers, searching together and walking in the same direction.

After his year in Trosly, Henri was invited to L'Arche Daybreak to become that community's pastor. The beginning of his time there was difficult. For one thing, Henri was not used to the demands of community life and was even less used to daily living in a house where sometimes he was asked to prepare breakfast, to wash dishes, to help people get up and dressed in the morning! He was not a particularly practical man. In addition, Henri's heart was not always quiet. He was still looking for, still needed, deep and lasting friendships.

It was both his beauty and his pain, this lifelong search for friendship. That which he most yearned for, he himself was ready to give—and to give fully! The most incredibly faithful and compassionate of friends, Henri was there whenever he felt that somebody needed him, and when he was there, he was prepared to give all his time and attention to that person. Henri lived to the letter the words of Jesus: "If someone asks you to walk a mile with him or her, walk two miles" (Matthew 5:41). He had a beautiful, compassionate heart, drawn to those who were in need.

Henri's cry for friendship and his faithfulness to friendship were particularly evident as he walked with people on their spiritual journeys. A wise and gentle spiritual guide, he led people closer to Jesus, to truth, to a greater acceptance of themselves and of reality. But he never imposed his faith or his ideas. He would listen to others and accept them as they were, and where they were, in their own human and spiritual paths. A total stranger could quickly become a friend: each day Henri received many letters; patient as well as thoughtful, he took the time to answer every one, sometimes at great length.

His own pain and anguish, his own thirst for understanding and friendship, gave Henri a deeper understanding of the yearnings, the loneliness, the needs of others. His wide knowledge of psychology and theology as well as matters of the spirit combined to make him an excellent counselor and spiritual guide.

Henri found his fullness in the Eucharist. He loved to celebrate the Eucharist and to include everybody in it, and if he sometimes seemed a bit casual with the rules of the Roman Catholic Church concerning intercommunion, it was because he wanted each one present to have a personal encounter with Jesus. Henri loved the Eucharist because he loved Jesus. And he believed passionately in the real presence of Jesus in the consecrated bread and wine. Because the Eucharist was of such great significance to him, he had a natural talent for making it meaningful, for showing its connectedness to our lives. He would circle the altar, walk out amongst the participants waving his hands here and there. Some people might have found these actions disturbing but they were all expressions of Henri's intense desire to bring people together, around Jesus.

Henri also loved the intimacy of the sacrament of reconciliation, where people open their hearts to a priest, show their deepest wounds, their sense of guilt, their anguish and their sinfulness, and where they hear the words "I forgive you in the name of the Father, the Son, and the Holy Spirit." Henri was truly a gentle instrument of a very loving, tender, and compassionate God.

But Henri was not the sort of person who relished obedience to authority, or to the institution of the church, or even to community structures. He was a good theologian who knew that Jesus was first and foremost interested in *people*. If Henri appeared to be a bit casual in respect to obedience, it was because he knew that his role as a priest was to be interested in people. But in many other ways Henri was quite traditional; he loved all the signs and symbols of the church; he loved the security that belonging to the church gave him; above all, he appreciated that this family of the church is one that honors love and prizes personal relationships.

Perhaps Henri would have preferred a more "motherly" church, filled with affection and tenderness. He was wary of the masculine authority in the church. At the same time, however, he yearned to be loved, admired, accepted, and confirmed by church authorities.

Part of Henri's need to belong showed itself in his dislike of conflict. Conflicts easily disturbed and stressed him, and he did everything to avoid them. And that is one of the reasons why, it seems to me, he had the charisma of a unifier. He chose to downplay differences, to overlook contradictions; he preferred cutting to the heart of situations and of people, finding there a deeper unity. By awakening hearts, helping people of different traditions to walk in their inner journeys, to meet Jesus, to rediscover trust in themselves, in their own creativity and intuition, Henri was amongst the great ecumenists of this century.

In some ways Henri was better known in the Protestant and Anglican communities than in his own church. Perhaps many in the Roman Catholic Church were slightly wary of him; he was clearly not very institutional.

Henri cried out for unity among Christians; the inner pain that he experienced as a result of the lack of unity among Christians could have been destructive for him. But he learned to channel the pain that flowed from his own sense of brokenness into bringing people from many churches together.

One of the gifts God gave Henri to help him fulfill his mission was the gift of writing. Henri was a compulsive writer. He *had* to write, and could become terribly sick and depressed if he couldn't channel his anguish and intuitions into clear, precisely written words. He struggled all the time with his writing; he would rewrite and rewrite his books, but he was never completely satisfied. Henri was Henri, obsessional in his perfectionism, a trait that could be quite unbearable for his community and his friends!

Anguish can, however, become an incredible source of energy, like gas that keeps the car running at full speed. Going where? One does not always know! And Henri's anguish and energy were easily misunderstood. Some people saw him as an impossible man, forever fighting with publishers for more artistic covers for his books, or for better translations, a man who was seeking personal recognition through his writings.

But what an incredible instrument of God!

People loved Henri's books because he wrote about spiritual things not as they *should be* but as they *are*. He knew how to describe his own mess as well as the mess of the world; at the same time he showed us how to discover the seeds of hope in it all.

The quality of Henri's intelligence allowed him to see the light in the little events of each day. That is why he was continually writing diaries. Sometimes he could be terribly indiscreet about people he had met; it never occurred to him that maybe they did not want to be in his books! At the same time a message flowed from these little events. And they were always intensely personal. Henri lived through a period of deep grief and depression. He fell into the pit of confusion, and at the lowest point his personality seemed to disintegrate. But he was not ashamed of this experience, and as a result he came out of it a better, more beautiful and compassionate man. By writing about this time (in *The Inner Voice of Love*) for all those who find themselves in the pit, or are terribly frightened of falling into it, Henri revealed a way of hope and resurrection. He rose from his own depression because of his faith in life and his trust in God. He clutched onto his faith or, rather, he let God clutch onto him.

I was always touched by Henri's honesty in relationships, and I was particularly touched by his honesty in his words and writings. He said and wrote as he felt and thought. In reality he was a very wounded man, but then aren't we all? Doesn't his beauty lie in the fact that he was able to recognize his own sense of woundedness, and then speak and write about it? The last thing anyone could accuse Henri of was hypocrisy. Yet God clearly used this man in all his brokenness to give life, to become a beacon of hope. Through his words and his writings, he knew how to meet people where they were. And so I believe he lived in a special way the sacrament of the word, touching people's hearts and bringing them from confusion to light. He was a wonderful, wonderful communicator, an extraordinary "wounded healer" whose legacy to us is a collection of words and books with healing power.

Henri's life was touched and changed because of his friendship with Adam Arnett, a man with disabilities who lived in the L'Arche Daybreak community. By coming to understand Adam, he experienced how the world is upside down in its quest for fame, fortune, and power. Henri was a gift to the Daybreak community and his friends at Daybreak continually inspired and refreshed him. Still, although he truly loved to be with the weak and the poor, he was unable to be with only them for long periods; he needed the stimulation of intellectual and spiritual friendships, and he needed time to write and to speak publicly.

When he was not writing, one way Henri dealt with being away from the community was to take Daybreak friends with him. He delighted in announcing the word with Bill Van Buren or Gord Henry at his side. The love springing from their brokenness helped him to bear and love his own brokenness. He in turn was very deeply loved by the men and women with disabilities in his community.

Through his talks and his books Henri became a public spokesperson for the mystery at the heart of L'Arche, proclaiming clearly the mystery of the Gospel message, the folly of the weak and the rejected as the secret and silent prophets of God.

The contradictions of the world were mirrored as always in the contradictions within Henri himself. On the one hand Henri was announcing the downward path as the place of truth, of healing, and of encountering Jesus. On the other hand he seemed obsessed by a need for public recognition, for acceptance in the world. Here again Henri lived out the contradictions that all of us experience, between Gospel values and worldly values, between what we say and what we actually live. That was his poverty. It is my poverty. It is the poverty of us all.

A final thought on Henri as a writer. One of his finest books is an analysis of the Rembrandt painting *The Return of the Prodigal Son* in the light of the Christian message. If Henri wrote about the prodigal son and the elder son, was it not because he recognized these two conflicting personalities, the irresponsible, radical son and the faithful, law-abiding son, deeply ingrained in himself? And did he not himself long for the all-loving and all-forgiving Father to receive him home? And did he not clearly recognize that his deepest struggle was to become like the Father, all-loving and all-accepting, expecting nothing of others?

Anguish did not close Henri up within himself; he did not seek shelter from the world for very long. On the contrary, anguish pushed him ever forward, toward the new: new people, new discussions, new insights, new books. He loved to be with circus performers, people with AIDS, teachers, politicians, to be with the great of the world as readily as with those who were rejected. He loved the world of art, culture, music, and theater. He loved all that is human. And in all things he sought the truth that he would one day put into a new book. At the end, I think, his desire to write new books was not just the desire for greater recognition but the burning desire of a prophet to announce the light that is already in the world.

John the Evangelist begins his Gospel with "In the beginning was the 'logos.'" Henri was an ardent searcher for the "logos," the meaning of all things, the secret light hidden in all things. It was this seeking for truth and for God that brought him to L'Arche. Somehow he had seen and experienced the mystery hidden in the weak and the broken. He had also discovered that healing cannot come to each one of us, to our communities, and to our broken societies unless we all take the downward path ourselves and with others.

The words that flowed from his brokenness, contradictions, and struggles—weaknesses he never hid—were healing words. Jesus says that a tree can be judged only by its fruits. The fruits of

Henri's life were numerous, good, and beautiful: he brought people to God, to the light, and to renewed hope.

And when he died in that hospital in Holland, he died a holy death. He had accepted poverty. He was ready to meet Jesus, whom he loved and sought all his life, and to whom he had given his life.

Letters from a Friendship

BILL VAN BUREN

Bill Van Buren was a founding member of L'Arche Daybreak in 1969. He works in the Woodery. Bill and Henri were close friends and enjoyed traveling together. In 1995, Henri wrote a letter for the book Bill was compiling about his life. As a contribution to this book, Bill asked Sue Mosteller to help him prepare his response to Henri's letter.

June 1995
Dear Bill,

You are my special friend at Daybreak. From the moment I came to Daybreak in August 1986 I have thought of you as a very special person that I would like to know better and that I would love to have as a friend. . . . Many people all over the world know that Bill and Henri are special friends and I am really proud of that. . . .

Our trip to Washington was really the beginning of many other trips we have made since. . . . You remember "the elevator event" [on our trip to Irvine, California]. You and I went into the elevator and there were many people standing against the walls not saying a word. As the elevator was moving upwards you broke the silence by saying to your neighbor, looking at his feet, "You could certainly use a shoeshine," and *when your neighbor grinned at your remark, you said, "But I certainly could use one too!" Within a few seconds everybody was talking to one another in such an animated way that people forgot to get off on the floors where they were supposed to get off. I always consider that little event a good example of creating community on the spot. . . .*

Although people often invite me to speak because of their hope to hear something about the spiritual life from me, they mostly remember me because of my coming with you. . . .

Now we are both becoming a little older and we both feel it. That is why you keep saying, "When I die first, Henri will be upset, and when Henri dies first, I will be upset. Maybe we should die together." With this little joke you remind me and yourself that we both will die one day but that we are friends for life and that God who brought us together will keep us together. . . .

You are a very special man and a very beautiful friend.

With love,

Henri

May 2000
Dear Henri,

I read the letter you wrote to me in my life-story book. It made me think of how we were best friends. Now I write a letter to you for your life-story book.

I remember when I was baptized. I said to you, "I want to be

Bill Van Buren and Henri.

baptized." You said to me, "You have to learn about it and I want you
to learn at the church so others can know you." I said, "OK." After my
baptism, I felt really happy. From then on, you accompanied me. That
means you helped me live a good life. I also accompanied you. That
means I helped you on your trips.

Before I met you no one ever asked me to go on a trip before. I was
excited. You asked me to go to Washington because you wanted us to go
together. You kept telling me that it was important for us to go together,
like brothers, and talk about our life at Daybreak. When you gave your
talk I wanted to say more about God and about our friendship, but you
held on to the microphone. I liked to tell jokes like "What do you call a
camel without a hump?" Dead silence! Then I gave the answer,
"Humphrey!" All the people cracked up at my jokes. You used to wave
your hands around when you were talking. But I liked to hear you and
sometimes when you talked I started to cry. I don't know why and I
couldn't help it because I felt so close to you. We were best friends.

You made me happy the day you blessed my life-story book. In the chapel you told me that my life was important and that many people loved me. No one ever told me that before. You said God loved me. I re-member when you blessed my book I started to cry and you had to hold me because I was shaking. I wish I had a picture of you blessing my life-story book. It touched me so much to hear what you said.

Thank you for taking me on trips. Thank you for the books and the pictures you gave me. They are on the wall in my room. I miss you, Henri, and I still cry for you. Thank you for being my best friend.

Love,

Bill

HANDS

When I went to St. Petersburg to see Rembrandt's *The Return of the Prodigal Son*, I had little idea how much I would have to live what I then saw. I stand with awe at the place where Rembrandt brought me. He led me from the kneeling, disheveled young son to the standing, bent-over father, from the place of being blessed to the place of blessing. As I look at my own aging hands, I know that they have been given me to stretch out towards all who suffer, to rest upon the shoulders of all who come, and to offer the blessing that emerges from the immensity of God's love.

—The Return of the Prodigal Son

The Henri Nouwen Literary Centre may be reached through
its Web site: *http://www.nouwen*, or by e-mail at
nouwencentre@nouwen.net.

Proceeds from the sale of this book will go to L'Arche Daybreak
for the work of the Dayspring, which supports projects in
keeping with Henri Nouwen's vision and interests.

Photo Credits

Cover; photo by Paula Kilcoyne
p. 11; photographer unknown, courtesy of The Nouwen Centre
p. 24; photo by Joe Child
p. 26; photo by Jack Stroh
p. 30; photo by Zoel Breau
p. 34; photo by Volker Seding
p. 37; photo by Carl MacMillan
p. 63; photographer unknown, used courtesy of The Nouwen Centre
p. 70; photographer unknown, used courtesy of The Nouwen Centre
p. 71; photographer unknown, used courtesy of The Nouwen Centre
p. 98; photo by Bob Buford
p. 100; photo by Paula Keleher
p. 104; photo by Jutta Ayer
p. 115; photo by Paula Keleher
p. 119; photo by Kathy Bruner
p. 127; photo by John Tolley
p. 150; photo by Ron van den Bosch
p. 162; photo by Robert Stamenov
p. 174; photo by Nathan Ball
p. 185; photo by Doug Wiebe
p. 203; photo by Jutta Ayer
p. 221; photo by Susan Steers
p. 228; photographer unknown, used courtesy of The Nouwen Centre
p. 240; photo by Wendy Lywood
p. 260; photographer unknown, used courtesy of The Nouwen Centre
p. 271; photo by Todd Rothrock

The Nouwen Centre and the Editors of this book have made every effort to identify and credit the photographers.

BETH PORTER is a lecturer in English and a freelance writer. She knew Henri Nouwen as a friend and colleague in the L'Arche Daybreak Community, where she has lived and worked for many years.

SUSAN M. S. BROWN worked closely with Henri Nouwen during 1995–96 and on his posthumously published books.

PHILIP COULTER worked with L'Arche's founder, Jean Vanier, on his bestselling book *Becoming Human*.